THE LIFE *of the* PARTY

FIRST IN THE SERIES

FROM

THE JUNIOR LEAGUE OF TAMPA

CULINARY COLLECTION

CREATORS OF

THE GASPARILLA COOKBOOK, A TASTE OF TAMPA, AND TAMPA TREASURES

To purchase copies of *The Life of the Party*, visit us online at www.jltampa.org, complete the order form in the back of this book, or call The Junior League of Tampa at 813-254-1734, extension 502.

Nothing brings people together like food. Whether it's a scent that conjures up fond childhood memories, comfort food offered as the salve that tempers our grief, or the right mix of food and drink that turns the most casual get-together into the party of the century, food is at the core of what connects us all.

The Life of the Party is the culmination of great recipes and festive inspirations with an emphasis on making your next entertaining venture a relaxing experience.

Our mantra in creating this book has been "no party is out of our reach." With skillful planning, creative make-ahead recipes, and fun menu suggestions, you might actually have time to take a shower, make a drink, and greet your guests at the door with a smile.

Entertaining is the perfect time to try new things. Our book embraces the attitude that cooks want to spend less time in the kitchen and more time with their guests— but not at the expense of their food or presentation. So come on in to our party . . . find some creative twists on classic recipes, new ideas that will wow your friends and family, and entertaining tips that we hope will inspire you to take on any party with vigor and enjoy each moment you spend with your guests.

—*The Life of the Party Committee*

THE LIFE of the PARTY

THE JUNIOR LEAGUE OF TAMPA
Culinary Collection

THE LIFE *of the* PARTY

Volume 1 of The Junior League of Tampa Culinary Collection

The Junior League of Tampa, Inc., is an organization of women committed to promoting voluntarism, developing the potential of women and improving communities through effective action and leadership of trained volunteers. Its purpose is exclusively educational and charitable.

Proceeds from the sale of this cookbook will be reinvested in the community through Junior League of Tampa projects.

The Junior League of Tampa, Inc.
87 Columbia Drive
Tampa, Florida 33606
813-254-1734

Copyright 2003 by
The Junior League of Tampa, Inc.

ISBN: 0-9609556-3-1
Library of Congress Number: 2002104801

Edited, Designed, and Manufactured by
Favorite Recipes® Press

FRP

P.O. Box 305142
Nashville, Tennessee 37230
800-358-0560

Book Design: David Malone
Art Director: Steve Newman
Project Editor: Ginger Dawson

Cover photograph generously underwritten by Mary Lee Nunnally Farrior

Manufactured in the United States of America
First Printing: 2003
25,000 copies

This cookbook is a collection of favorite recipes,
which are not necessarily original recipes.

MAJOR CONTRIBUTORS

Special thanks to our major contributors for their gracious support of
THE LIFE *of the* PARTY

HSN
Food Stylists provided by HSN

BERN'S FAMILY OF LEGENDS
Bern's Steak House / SideBern's / Bern's Fine Wines & Spirits
Wine tips provided by Head Sommelier Ken Collura

NEIMAN MARCUS, INTERNATIONAL PLAZA
Tableware shown in photographs throughout our book courtesy of Neiman Marcus
Please see the back of the book for information on how to obtain props used in photos throughout the book.

COOKBOOK PHOTOGRAPHY—Robert Adamo
FOOD STYLISTS—Debra Murray, Tracy Krause, John Viereck
SET STYLIST—Jodi Muller
FLORIST—Floral Impressions, Inc., Harrison Giddens
THE JUNIOR LEAGUE OF TAMPA CULINARY COLLECTION LOGO—
Atlas Advertising and Design, Christy Atlas

COOKBOOK DEVELOPMENT COMMITTEE

CHAIRMAN
Danielle Welsh

SUSTAINER ADVISOR / CO-CHAIRMAN
Kristie Salzer

Lynn Stanford, Photography • Elizabeth Harris, Recipe Testing
Maryanne McDonough, Art / Design • Mimi Obeck, Tasting Events
Cheryl Benitez • Dara Leslie • Lauren Stallings • Teresa Weachter
Nancy Harvey Mynard, President 2002–2003 • Mindy Murphy, President 2001–2002

THE LIFE OF THE PARTY TESTING CAPTAINS
Lisa Andrews • Cheryl Benitez • Cynthia Hahmann
Teresa Weachter • Missy Weiner

THE LIFE OF THE PARTY SPECIAL EVENTS CAPTAINS
Tracy McBride • Angie Sparks

CHAPTER PHOTO SPONSORSHIPS

Front Cover Image—THE LIFE OF THE PARTY—Mary Lee Farrior

Chapter One—PARTIES

This photograph was generously underwritten by The JLT Presidents from the 1970s including Ruthanne McLean, Ordy Hendry, Ann Murphey, Betty Ann Jordan, Mary Hill Gould, Mia C. Hardcastle, Joanne H. Frazier, Adajean Samson, Barbara B. Romano, and Stella Ferguson Thayer.

Chapter Two—PRELUDES

This photograph was generously underwritten by The JLT Presidents from the 1980s including Sandra Ott Gardner, Penelope P. Herman, June Sutton Annis, Rosemary Henderson, Gwynne A. Young, Becky Bell Savitz, and Susan Durand Thomas.

Chapter Three—SIDELINERS

This photograph was generously underwritten by The JLT Presidents from the 1990s including Robin W. DeLaVergne, Julianne McKeel, Hilary Howell Davis, Cindy Daley Coney, Karen Ryals, Becky Black Charles, Gwyn Schabacker, Patty Power Bohannan, Mary McKeever Merryday, and Betsy Wood Chambers.

Chapter Four—MAIN EVENTS

This photograph was generously underwritten by The JLT Past Sustainer Presidents including Louise Lykes Ferguson, Helen A. Davis, Martha Carlton Ward, Jane Price Watson, Carroll Cone Cozart Saxton, Pat Turner Daley, Ellen H. McLean, Laura Mickler Bentley, and Susan Bulger.

Chapter Five—GRAND FINALES

This photograph was generously underwritten by The JLT Presidents from the 2000s including Barbara Harvey Ryals, Lauren Cordell Stallings, Mindy Smith Murphy, Nancy Harvey Mynard, and Lisa Cave Andrews.

Menu Photo Sponsorships

Dinner Club

This photograph was generously underwritten by The JLT Past Sustainer Presidents including Judy Lawson, Bonnie H. Judy, Mary Audrey Whitehurst Wilson, Harrison Giddens, Helen Thompson Kerr, Sharon Smith Pizzo, Nell Ward, Barbara Pieper, Marie Preston, and Lesley Dobbins.

Beach Bash

This photograph was generously underwritten by Ferman Motor Car Company.

Baby Shower

This photograph was generously underwritten by Tampa General Hospital.

Gasparilla Brunch

This photograph was generously underwritten by Laura Mickler Bentley.

Football Fare

This photograph was generously underwritten by The JLT Past Sustainer Presidents including Isabelle Swift Ferrell, Jane Hughey Hewit, Lora Warren Hulse, Camille O. Thomas, Sherrill O'Neal, Sue Isbell, Anna Boswell, Jean Samson Suringa, and Carole Roberts Fields.

Countdown to Cocktails

This photograph was generously underwritten by Northern Trust.

Girls' Night Out

This photograph was generously underwritten by The JLT Presidents from the 1950s and 1960s including Jane Hall Witt, Martha Sale Ferman, Mary S. Wolfe, Sue W. McNevin, Martha R. Hall, Peggy Walker Sumner, Betsy McMichael Gilmore, Dada Pittman, Jane Duke Taylor, Jean Ann Cone, and Helen Coles Price.

WOMEN BUILDING BETTER COMMUNITIES

 Junior League of Tampa cookbooks have always served as a legacy, an investment of time and tradition, handed from one generation to another, from our community to yours. But more than that, Junior League of Tampa cookbooks are an investment in the foundation of our community.

Since 1926, the volunteers in our organization have shared their time, talent, and treasures with the city of Tampa. Here is a glimpse of some of the projects and organizations that we have been proud to support through volunteer hours and money raised through fundraisers including the sale of our cookbooks.

Adoption Picnics for Special Needs Children
Alpha House, A Home for Pregnant Women
Child Abuse Council
Children's Cancer Center
FunBook/ FunCart for Hospitalized Children
Guardian Ad Litem
Habitat for Humanity
H. Lee Moffitt Hospital & Cancer Research Institute
Immunization Promotional Campaign
Lifepath Hospice Circle of Love Bereavement Camp
Lowry Park Zoo
Metropolitan Ministries Day Care Center
Minority Youth Leadership Program for Girls
MORE Health, An Educational Program for Schoolchildren
Recycling Made Easy
Ronald McDonald House
Tampa Bay Performing Arts Center
Tampa General Hospital Sunshine House
The Children's Literacy Project
The Children's Museum of Tampa & Kid City
The Learning Lab: A Florida Aquarium Outreach Program
The Spring of Tampa Bay, A Domestic Violence Shelter
Thumbs Up for Child Safety
YMCA Daycare Resource and Referral Service

Contents

PARTIES

DINNER CLUB

MENU

CHIC COSMOPOLITANS

GOAT CHEESE MARINARA WITH
HERB TOAST

SAUSAGE BLOSSOMS

CHAMPAGNE SALMON PACKAGES

CITRUS AND GREENS WITH
SALAD DRESSING TO-DIE-FOR

PESTO GREEN BEANS

MOLTEN CHOCOLATE LAVA CAKES

AFTER-DINNER MARTINIS

A Dinner Club can be as elegant as a four-course meal served on fine china at the water's edge or as outrageous as a themed party that brings even the shyest couple out of their shells.

SOME IDEAS TO CONSIDER IF YOU ARE STARTING A DINNER CLUB:

• For a more formal, intimate dinner club, six couples is usually a good number both to promote good conversation and to comfortably seat around a dining room table.

• If you are having trouble limiting your invitation list, have two couples act as hosts.

• Choosing couples that live in close proximity sometimes works better because it increases the likelihood of participation.

• Try to meet consistently—once a month or every six weeks. Rotate homes to give everyone the opportunity to play host.

• Let the host choose the theme, supply the main course, and assign accompaniments.

• BYOB—this way everyone enjoys what they like to drink. The host can provide a signature drink.

For guaranteed laughs, go all out! Work your invitations, decorations, food, menu, dress, music, everything around your theme.

HERE ARE SOME IDEAS THAT HAVE PROVEN TO BE SUCCESSFUL:

• 1970s—Hit your local thrift store for great clothes, shoes, and disco balls.

• Scavenger Hunt—Give everyone a Polaroid camera and send them out with clues.

• Mexican—Host a Cinco de Mayo party poolside with a variety of margarita flavors.

• Year-on-the-Road—Meet your group at different restaurants throughout the year.

• Olympics—Plan interactive games, have a big screen TV, and use flags of many nations as decorations.

• Other Ideas—Try a Newlywed Game, Key West Sunset or Hawaiian theme, Mystery Game, Halloween, Karaoke, or Western theme.

BEACH BASH

MENU

GARDEN SANGRIA

GAZPACHO BLANCO

BLACK BEAN VEGETABLE WRAPS

GRILLED SWORDFISH WITH
CITRUS SALSA

CORN ROASTED IN ROMAINE

SWEET AND SALTY TOMATO SALAD

CARAMEL PECAN BROWNIES

LIME MACADAMIA BARS

Whether you have access to a beach or you're importing the sand to make your own beach, this is the perfect party venue. A beach picnic is a classic way to enjoy the beauty of the outdoors—just beware of uninvited seagulls that may join your party.

Our Beach Bash menu includes grilled items, but if you don't have a portable grill, there are many substitutions you can make from our recipes.

HERE ARE A FEW REMINDERS TO MAKE YOUR NEXT BEACH PARTY A HIT:

• Keep your food cool—food spoils quickly in hot weather, so be sure to keep a cooler nearby to store food.

• If you're not limiting your menu to pick-up food, don't forget the utensils! Cups are essential, too.

• Choose a menu that makes sense for your surroundings—pick-up food is often much easier to eat at the beach (skewers, wraps, fruit, or bars make a good choice).

• Festive plates (especially disposable!) and tableware can help set the gala mood of your party.

• Don't forget the sunscreen and bug spray—nothing ruins a beach party like sunburns and bug bites.

• Bring garbage bags and wet wipes for a quick cleanup so that you can enjoy the rest of your day.

• If your party is going to last past sunset, don't forget candles and lots of matches or a lighter.

• Bring a volleyball and net, football, and frisbees for fun.

• What's a beach party without music? Remember batteries for the radio or CD player.

BABY SHOWER

MENU

MOCHACCINO PUNCH

CITRUS SLUSH

PESTO COCKTAIL WAFERS

CHICKEN BOURSIN BUNDLES

ASPARAGUS PECAN STACK

FESTIVAL STRAWBERRY SALAD

PEACHES AND BERRIES WITH CREAMY

GRAND MARNIER SAUCE

Welcoming a new baby into the world is a long-standing tradition that has become another opportunity for a soirée. This celebration can be girls-only, but a couple's shower to include the dad-to-be has gained popularity over the years.

SOME FUN DECORATING IDEAS FOR A BABY SHOWER:

• Place baby photos of the expectant parents throughout the house or use their pictures in frames as centerpieces on your buffet table. These are always good for a laugh.

• Place silver baby cups with cut fresh flowers at each place setting.

• Use baby quilts as table toppers over white tablecloths.

• Roll up pretty rickrack-decorated washcloths or burp cloths in silver teething rings or tie with raffia to use as the napkins for the party.

• Scatter pacifiers, pacifier clips, baby rattles, and other useful small items around your buffet table like confetti and then give them to mom-to-be.

TRY THESE NEW IDEAS INSTEAD OF TRADITIONAL:

• "I Owe You" Shower—Guests bring a recipe or an offer to do something for the couple after the baby arrives instead of a gift. Then in the weeks following the delivery, guests are scheduled to prepare the recipe/dinner for the new baby's family or perform the task offered (grocery shop, take siblings for the day, or do laundry).

• "Stock the Changing Table"—Guests bring receiving blankets, onesies, diapers, wipes, and any other essentials for the new addition.

• Dinner's on Us—Frozen casseroles for the family are the gifts for this shower. This gives the family lots of easy meals to thaw and eat once the baby arrives.

• Sip 'n See—This is a less gift-oriented shower idea that is great for a mother expecting her second or third child. Guests come at an appointed time after the baby is born (usually afternoon tea or brunch) to meet the new baby, minimizing the onslaught of drop-in visitors that can tire a new mother.

GASPARILLA BRUNCH

MENU

PIRATE'S MILK PUNCH

BERRY CRUMB CAKE

BRIE AND SAUSAGE BRUNCH SOUFFLÉ

ARROZ CON POLLO SALAD

MARINATED TOMATOES

SWEET ALMOND SQUARES

February in Tampa marks the start of Gasparilla—Tampa's signature event celebrating the fictional lore of old about a swashbuckler named Gaspar and his crew who sailed into Tampa Bay to plunder the city's treasures.

Every year hundreds of thousands of people gather to watch pirates in makeup and elaborate costumes invade the city on decorated pirate ships and boats, then parade down Tampa's magnificent Bayshore Boulevard.

In the whirlwind of parties, one rivals the next as the citizens of Tampa gather for pirates' feasts.

No matter what tradition you are celebrating, a brunch is always a nice way to gather people. And nothing caps off a great meal or brightens up a brunch like a coffee bar.

HERE ARE SOME COFFEE BAR TIPS:

• The experts say use two tablespoons of ground coffee for every six ounces of water. Use fresh ground coffee beans and fresh cold water for best results.

• Serve coffee in thermal containers. This will keep the coffee warm for hours.

• Stock the coffee bar with flavored syrups and liqueurs such as Kahlúa and Irish Cream.

• Serve both decaf and caffeinated coffee.

• Offer ground cinnamon and cocoa in shakers.

• Make sure there are plenty of teaspoons or swizzle sticks and cocktail napkins.

• Don't forget the basics such as cream and sugar, and the not-so-basic whipped cream.

FOOTBALL FARE

MENU

HOT SWISS BACON DIP

SASSY SALSA WITH BLUE CORN CHIPS

WHITE BEAN CHICKEN CHILI

PULLED PARTY PORK

GUACAMOLE SALAD

FROSTED PEANUT BUTTER BROWNIES

DOUBLE–CHOCOLATE
SHORTBREAD COOKIES

Football season conjures up thoughts of your favorite team's colors, gathering friends and rivals to watch the big games, and eating hearty satisfying food that makes you sigh and pat your belly. Sound like the makings of a great party? It is the perfect time to kick off the season.

Encourage your guests to wear team colors and then follow suit with the team paraphernalia you use to decorate. This can be one of the easiest decorating jobs—pom-poms, hats, helmets, banners, even your food can take on the team colors.

Set out food that is plentiful, easy to eat and easy to prepare ahead. Dips and pick-up appetizers like chicken wings and ribs are traditional favorites. Try hearty sandwiches like our Pulled Party Pork or Tailgate Roast Beef Sandwiches—they are easy to make ahead for a crowd and will leave your guests satisfied. Whatever the crowd, a buffet is often the best option so that your fans can keep coming back for more.

Roll in a big screen television or place multiple TV sets around your house and out on a porch. This spreads the party out and gives antsy football fans the opportunity to move around and release nervous energy.

HERE ARE SOME BUFFET BASICS:

Set the buffet up somewhere other than the dining room. Porches, sideboards, and kitchen islands can be excellent areas to set the stage. Let the season, occasion, or guest list direct you.

Use a variety of platters and serving pieces. Place platters of food at different heights on the buffet table. Books and boxes stacked under tablecloths provide height and interest. Layer the table with coordinating fabrics and interesting textures.

Set the food on the table in the order you would serve a sit-down meal. Buffet plates go at the beginning and napkins and utensils (tied together with ribbon or napkin rings) go at the end of the line.

Countdown To Cocktails

Do you feel overwhelmed when thinking about planning a party? We've provided this countdown to help break it down into more manageable steps to fit a party of any size and scope.

2 TO 3 WEEKS BEFORE:
- Send out invitations.
- Determine if you will need any rentals (tables, linens, glassware).
- Arrange for professional help to serve or clean.

1 WEEK BEFORE:
- Choose serving pieces.
- Polish the silver.
- Determine your centerpieces and order flowers or materials.
- Buy wine, champagne, liquor, and mixers.
- Organize a grocery list.
- Shop for nonperishables, including candles or sterno for chafing dishes.
- Prepare and freeze any freezable recipe.
- Select music for the party.

MENU

PEACH CHAMPAGNE COCKTAIL

BLUE CASHEW SPREAD

WARM CRAB DIP

GRILLED MARINATED SHRIMP

ASSORTED CROSTINI

TROPICAL LAYER BARS

LIME MACADAMIA BARS

BUTTER PECAN TARTS

2 DAYS BEFORE:
- Shop for perishables.

1 DAY BEFORE:
- Remove any frozen items from the freezer and thaw in the refrigerator.
- Set up the bar and buy the ice. Chill the wine and Champagne.
- Prepare the tables and set out serving platters.

PARTY DAY:
- Assemble garnishes for the bar.
- Arrange and set out flowers and candles.

1 TO 2 HOURS BEFORE PARTY:
- Place desserts on platters and garnish with fresh flowers, herbs, or whole nuts.
- Get dressed!

JUST BEFORE THE GUESTS ARRIVE:
- Fill ice bucket with ice.
- Set out food and drinks.
- Smile—you're the life of your party!

GIRLS' NIGHT OUT

MENU

WINE PUNCH

BUNCO JUMBLE

HOT AND SPICY SPINACH DIP

PARTY STEAK SPIRAL

MIXED GREENS WITH

BALSAMIC VINAIGRETTE

PAPAS CON MOJO

MACADAMIA CHEESECAKE

When the stress of daily life has got you maxed out, there is nothing like a girls' night out. Bunco and a book club are great ways to stay connected with friends and enjoy good food.

Bunco is a quick-rolling dice game usually played with a group of 12 or more, divided into tables of four. This fast-paced game keeps you hopping from table to table and playing for a score of 21—which is Bunco.

Although there are several versions of the game, the most basic has you changing partners every round, which keeps the conversation lively and often disjointed!

A warning though—this is not your mother's bridge club.

ALL PRECONCEPTIONS ASIDE, BUNCO IS MORE LIKE A MEN'S POKER PARTY WITH THREE DIFFERENCES:
- You play with dice.
- You eat great food.
- You often have to dodge long, sharp fingernails.

BOOK CLUBS ARE ALSO A BIG HIT FOR GIRLS' NIGHT OUT. THEY CAN BE ORGANIZED IN A VARIETY OF WAYS:
- Meet in the morning for coffee and brunch.
- Meet in the evening for dessert and drinks.
- Theme your book clubs, using the book to dictate the kind of food that is served. For instance, a book on the South lends itself to a southern menu.
- Make it a book club/dinner club where the hostess makes the main course and everyone brings accompaniments.
- After drinks and appetizers, the group meets around the table for the main course and discussion of the book.
- Alternate between members' homes allowing everyone a chance to play hostess.
- Plan one night's theme around a favorite cookbook. Try to choose a cookbook with a specific theme such as Asian, Vegetarian, or the Florida Coast!

PRELUDES

YELLOWFIN TUNA SPRING ROLLS

When you want a showstopper, try this creative appetizer from Chef Jeannie Pierola. Jeannie is Chef/Partner at the celebrated SideBern's restaurant and Executive Chef/Culinary Director at Bern's Steak House. Her "One World Cuisine" has earned her national acclaim and a loyal following.

SPRING ROLLS

1 pound sushi-grade tuna	1 cucumber, julienned
8 sheets rice paper	1 avocado, thinly sliced
2 cups cooked somen noodles	Cilantro leaves
1 cup julienned carrot	Mint leaves
3 scallions, julienned	

PEANUT DIPPING SAUCE

1 (14-ounce) can coconut milk	1/2 ounce sambal chili paste
1 cup sweet soy sauce or tamari	1/2 ounce fish sauce
1 teaspoon sesame oil	1 1/2 cups creamy peanut butter
1 teaspoon chopped garlic	Juice of 3 limes

TAMARI LIME DIPPING SAUCE

3/4 cup tamari or soy sauce	1 teaspoon sesame oil
1/3 cup rice wine vinegar	1 teaspoon chili flakes
2 garlic cloves, minced	Juice of 2 limes

For the spring rolls, cut the tuna into 1/2×2-inch strips. Soak the rice paper in a bowl of room temperature water until softened; remove to a damp cloth. Place a slice of tuna in the middle of a piece of rice paper. Top with a small amount of noodles, carrot, scallions, cucumber, a slice of avocado, cilantro and mint. Working quickly, fold the top and sides of the rice paper and roll up tightly. Place the finished roll on a serving plate, seam side down, and cover with a damp cloth. Repeat for the remaining rolls. Serve immediately with the Peanut Dipping Sauce or Tamari Lime Dipping Sauce.

For the peanut sauce, combine the coconut milk, sweet soy, sesame oil, garlic, sambal and fish sauce in a saucepan. Heat until the mixture is hot, but not boiling. Stir in the peanut butter and lime juice until well blended. Cool to room temperature before serving.

For the lime sauce, combine the tamari, rice wine vinegar, garlic, sesame oil, chili flakes and lime juice in a bowl. Whisk until well blended. Chill, covered, until serving time.

Yield: 8 spring rolls

LOBSTER QUESADILLAS WITH MANGO SALSA

Succulent lobster and a cool and spicy salsa team up to make this an unforgettable appetizer.
This recipe is courtesy of Robert Lugo, Executive Chef of Northern Trust. Under his direction,
the Bank's private Executive dining room has become a sought-after reservation.

QUESADILLAS
4 (9-inch) flour tortillas
2/3 cup shredded Monterey Jack cheese
1/3 cup shredded Pepper Jack cheese
2 boiled lobster tails, chopped into bite-size pieces
1/2 yellow onion, chopped
3 tablespoons chopped scallions
2 tablespoons chopped red bell pepper
1/4 cup vegetable oil

MANGO SALSA
4 ripe mangoes, chopped
1 bunch fresh cilantro, chopped
1 red onion, chopped
1/2 red bell pepper, chopped
1/2 fresh pineapple, chopped
1 teaspoon salt, or to taste
1/2 teaspoon Tabasco sauce
Juice of 1 lime

For the quesadillas, place 1 tortilla on a work surface. Sprinkle with a layer of Monterey Jack cheese and Pepper Jack cheese. Add a layer of lobster, onion, scallions and bell pepper. Top with another layer of the cheeses. Cover with another tortilla. Heat the oil in a skillet until hot. Add the prepared quesadilla. Cook until brown on the bottom, flip over carefully and cook until brown on the other side and the cheese is melted. Remove to a plate and cut into individual pieces. Repeat with the remaining tortillas and filling ingredients. Serve with the Mango Salsa.

For the salsa, combine the mangoes, cilantro, onion, bell pepper, pineapple, salt, Tabasco sauce and lime juice in a bowl and mix well. Season to taste if necessary. Chill, covered, until serving time.

Yield: 8 to 12 servings

GRILLED MARINATED SHRIMP

Simple, divine, and always a hit. For a different presentation that is also aromatic, thread the shrimp on the woody end of rosemary branches, leaving some of the leaves on the end.

1/2 cup vegetable or canola oil
1/4 cup soy sauce
1/4 cup lemon juice
2 tablespoons chopped fresh gingerroot
2 garlic cloves, minced
2 pounds fresh jumbo shrimp, peeled, deveined

Combine the oil, soy sauce, lemon juice, gingerroot and garlic in a bowl and mix well. Add the shrimp to the mixture, tossing to mix well. Chill, covered, for 2 to 3 hours. Thread the shrimp onto skewers. Grill over hot coals for 3 to 4 minutes on each side or until the shrimp turn pink. If using wooden skewers, soak in water for 15 minutes.

Yield: 8 to 10 servings

RAISING THE BAR

Bar basics for cocktail parties: Plan on three to four drinks per person;
one (750-milliliter) bottle of liquor makes about 25 drinks.
There are five to six glasses of wine in a standard bottle. For a full bar, you need:
two bottles of vodka; one bottle each of gin and scotch; several bottles of
mixers such as vermouth, club soda, tonic water, and fruit juice;
garnishes such as citrus wedges, coarse salt, olives, cocktail onions, and cherries;
swizzle sticks, bottle openers, corkscrew, cocktail shaker, and jigger;
plenty of glasses; ice; and cocktail napkins.

GROUPER CAKES WITH TARTAR SAUCE

This is a Florida take on the ever-popular crab cake. This member was inspired to create these after her husband had a fruitful day of fishing. These may be prepared ahead of time and reheated before serving.

GROUPER CAKES

2 tablespoons butter
2 tablespoons olive oil
1 1/2 cups finely chopped celery
3/4 cup finely chopped red onion
1/2 cup finely chopped red bell pepper
1/4 cup minced fresh parsley
1 tablespoon capers, drained
1 teaspoon Creole seasoning
1/2 teaspoon Worcestershire sauce

1/2 teaspoon Tabasco sauce
1/2 teaspoon salt
1/2 teaspoon freshly ground pepper
1/2 pound grouper fillet, baked
1/2 cup dry bread crumbs or crushed butter crackers
1/2 cup mayonnaise
2 teaspoons Dijon mustard
2 eggs, lightly beaten
Olive oil for frying

TARTAR SAUCE

1/2 cup mayonnaise
3 tablespoons finely chopped pickles
2 tablespoons coarse-grain mustard

2 or 3 tablespoons white wine vinegar
Salt and freshly ground pepper to taste

For the grouper cakes, heat the butter and 2 tablespoons olive oil in a skillet over medium heat. Sauté the celery, onion, bell pepper, parsley and capers for 15 minutes or until tender. Stir in the Creole seasoning, Worcestershire sauce, Tabasco sauce, salt and pepper. Remove from the heat and let cool. Flake the grouper into a large bowl. Stir in the bread crumbs, mayonnaise, Dijon mustard and beaten eggs. Fold in the celery mixture just until combined. Chill, covered, for 30 minutes. Shape into small cakes. Heat the olive oil in a large skillet. Sauté the grouper cakes until golden brown on each side. Remove to paper towels to drain. Serve hot with the Tartar Sauce.

For the tartar sauce, combine the mayonnaise, pickles, coarse-grain mustard, white wine vinegar, salt and pepper in a bowl and mix well. Chill, covered, until serving time.

Yield: 24 appetizer cakes or 12 entrée cakes

SMOKED SALMON BRUSCHETTA WITH FENNEL AND GOAT CHEESE

This recipe came to us from Chef Marty Blitz of the acclaimed Mise en Place Restaurant.
Chef Blitz is known for innovative combinations highlighting local ingredients and culture.

4 ounces thinly sliced smoked salmon
1 fennel bulb, sliced
1 small red onion, thinly sliced
Zest of 1/2 lemon
1/4 cup olive oil
Salt to taste
Pepper to taste
2 tablespoons olive oil
8 (1/3-inch-thick) slices French baguette
1 ounce goat cheese
2 tablespoons heavy cream

Combine the salmon, fennel, onion, lemon zest and 1/4 cup olive oil in a small bowl and mix well. Season with salt and pepper; set aside.

Drizzle 2 tablespoons olive oil over the baguette slices. Grill the bread over hot coals until light brown and grill marks appear. You may also toast under a broiler. Remove to a serving platter.

Combine the goat cheese and cream in a small bowl. Mix well with a wooden spoon until very smooth. Top the grilled bread slices with a spoonful of the salmon mixture. Spoon the goat cheese mixture over the top. You may garnish with the feathery tops of the fennel bulb or sprigs of fresh dill if desired. Serve immediately.

Yield: 8 slices

TAILGATE ROAST BEEF ON ROLLS

We promise there will be no leftovers of these savory sandwiches after you serve them.
You may prepare these ahead and wrap in foil until ready to bake.

8 ounces cream cheese, softened
1 envelope ranch salad dressing mix
1/2 cup chopped green onions
1 (24-count) package small dinner rolls
1 to 2 pounds deli-sliced Cajun roast beef
12 slices Swiss cheese
1/2 cup (1 stick) butter, melted

Combine the cream cheese, ranch dressing mix and green onions in a small bowl and mix well.
Remove rolls from the package. Slice the rolls horizontally; remove the top of the rolls in one piece.
Spread the mixture on the cut side of both layers. Layer the roast beef and Swiss cheese slices on
the bottom layer. Cover with the top layer of rolls; brush with the melted butter. Arrange on a baking
sheet. Bake at 350 degrees for 10 to 15 minutes or until golden brown. Slice into 24 small rolls.
Serve warm.

Yield: 12 servings

INVITATION ETIQUETTE

With today's technology at our fingertips, invitations are easier

than ever to create. Whether you do the invitations yourself or have

them professionally printed, here are a few tips for doing it right:

For formal dinner parties, invitations should be in the mail at least

three weeks before the event. For casual gatherings, a phone call is

fine. Reserve e-mail invitations for only the closest of friends

and most informal gatherings. Clever poems and rhyming phrases are

a fun way to make your invitations catchier.

SAUSAGE BITES IN BOURBON SAUCE

*This dish is even better when allowed to marinate overnight in the refrigerator
before baking. This is something that can be served casually in front of the television or
elegantly in a silver chafing dish on a buffet table.*

3 pounds smoked link sausage
1 cup packed brown sugar

1 cup each bourbon and chili
sauce

Slice the sausage into bite-size pieces and place in a baking dish. Combine the brown sugar,
bourbon and chili sauce in a bowl and mix well. Pour over the sausage, stirring to coat well. Bake,
covered, at 325 degrees for 2 hours and 30 minutes. Serve hot in a chafing dish with wooden picks.
You may combine the sausage and sauce 1 day in advance and marinate in the refrigerator until needed.

Yield: 8 to 12 servings

SAUSAGE BLOSSOMS

*Won ton wrappers make this appetizer a snap to put together. The wrappers look like flower
petals or blossoms, creating a pretty cup to hold the spicy sausage and cheese mixture.*

2 pounds Italian sausage,
casings removed
2 cups shredded Colby
Jack cheese

2 cups salsa
1 package won ton wrappers
Sour cream
Chopped green onions

Brown the sausage in a skillet, stirring until crumbly. Remove from the heat and add the Colby
Jack cheese and salsa, stirring until the cheese is melted. Press the won ton wrappers into miniature
muffin cups, leaving the edges extending upward. Spoon a heaping tablespoon of the sausage mixture
into each cup. Bake at 350 degrees for 10 minutes or until won ton edges begin to brown. Remove to a
serving platter and let stand for 5 minutes. Spoon a small amount of sour cream on top of each sausage
blossom and sprinkle with chopped green onions. Serve immediately.

Yield: 24 appetizers

STROMBOLI WITH MUSTARD DIPPING SAUCE

Using a prepared pizza crust makes this quick to make and quick to disappear. Serve hot or cold as an appetizer or an entrée. We also tried this with pepperoni and sausage for a spicier version.

STROMBOLI
1 (10-ounce) can refrigerated pizza dough
1/4 teaspoon basil
1/3 pound thinly sliced ham
1 1/2 pounds (6 cups) shredded mozzarella cheese
1 egg, beaten
1 garlic clove, minced

MUSTARD DIPPING SAUCE
1/4 cup prepared yellow mustard
1/4 cup Dijon mustard
1/4 cup coarse-grain mustard
1/2 teaspoon dried mixed herbs, crushed

For the stromboli, roll out the pizza dough onto a work surface. Sprinkle with the basil. Cover the dough with the ham slices, leaving 1/4 of the edge uncovered. Sprinkle with the mozzarella cheese. Roll up lengthwise and place, seam side down, on a greased baking sheet. Combine the egg and garlic in a small bowl. Brush the top of the dough with the egg mixture. Bake at 350 degrees for 35 to 40 minutes or until golden brown. Let cool. Cut the stromboli into 1 1/2-inch pieces and serve with the Mustard Dipping Sauce.

For the sauce, combine the yellow mustard, Dijon mustard and coarse-grain mustard in a bowl and mix well. Stir in the herbs.

Yield: 4 servings

PESTO COCKTAIL WAFERS

We added pesto flavors for a fresh approach to a southern favorite, the cheese wafer.
These pair well with cocktails and other hors d'oeuvres. The wrapped logs can be frozen for up to a
month so you can have appetizers on hand for last-minute gatherings.

1 1/2 cups shredded Cheddar cheese	1/8 teaspoon white pepper
1/2 cup (1 stick) butter, softened	1 cup fresh basil leaves
1 cup flour	1/2 cup pine nuts
1/4 teaspoon cayenne pepper	1/2 cup grated Parmesan cheese
	1 garlic clove

Combine the cheese, butter, flour and peppers in a medium bowl and stir until well mixed, or alternately, mix in a food processor and then remove to a medium bowl. Combine the basil, pine nuts, Parmesan cheese and garlic in a food processor. Process until well mixed and pine nuts are minced. Add to the cheese mixture and mix well.

Shape the dough into 2 logs. Wrap in plastic wrap and refrigerate for several hours or until firm. Cut into 1/8-inch slices and place on a parchment-lined baking sheet. Bake at 350 degrees for 10 to 12 minutes or until edges are golden brown.

Yield: 2 dozen wafers

WINE AT COCKTAIL PARTIES

The best wines for parties are light and easy drinking, never heavy
or tannic. For whites, try Pinot Grigio from Italy or Sauvignon
Blanc from New Zealand. For reds, nothing beats Pinot Noir for
flexibility. Try something from Oregon or California or maybe a
Beaujolais from France. Serve these reds cool.

TOMATO PARMESAN CROSTINI

We have enjoyed plenty of crostini before, but had never seen one with a rich Parmesan spread.
This is a great recipe to showcase yellow or heirloom tomatoes.

4 to 5 plum tomatoes,
finely chopped
2 to 3 garlic cloves, minced
2 tablespoons chopped fresh basil
1/4 cup olive oil
Salt to taste

Pepper to taste
1/2 cup grated Parmesan cheese
1/2 cup mayonnaise
1 loaf French bread, sliced into
1/2-inch rounds

Combine the tomatoes, garlic, basil, olive oil, salt and pepper in a bowl and mix well; set aside.
Mix the Parmesan cheese and mayonnaise in a small bowl. Spread on the bread rounds. Place the
bread rounds on a baking sheet. Top each bread round with a spoonful of the tomato mixture. Bake at
400 degrees for 10 minutes or until bubbly.

Yield: 8 servings

WINE PRIMER

Wines have different textures and weights. Light whites: Albarino
from Spain, Sancerre from the Loire Valley. Medium whites: Pinot
Gris from Oregon, Riesling from Alsace. Heavy whites:
Chardonnay from California. Light reds: Beaujolais and Pinot Noir.
Medium reds: Merlot, Rioja from Spain. Heavy reds:
Cabernet Sauvignon, Syrah, or Zinfandel.

ANTIPASTO TORTA

All the flavors of an antipasto selection in a colorful presentation for your table.

1 (3-ounce) package sun-dried tomatoes
1 (14-ounce) can diced tomatoes
3/4 onion, chopped
1 tablespoon minced garlic
2 tablespoons olive oil
2 bay leaves
1/2 teaspoon sugar
1/4 teaspoon basil
8 ounces cream cheese, softened
2 tablespoons butter or margarine, softened
1/2 cup grated Parmesan cheese
2 teaspoons prepared pesto
9 slices Muenster or mozzarella cheese

Soften the sun-dried tomatoes in a bowl of boiling water for 20 minutes; drain and coarsely chop. Drain the can of tomatoes, reserving 1/4 cup of the juice. Sauté the onion and garlic in the olive oil in a skillet for 4 minutes or until tender. Stir in the diced tomatoes, reserved tomato juice, bay leaves, sugar and basil. Bring to a boil, reduce the heat and simmer for 3 to 5 minutes or until thickened. Remove from the heat. Discard the bay leaves and stir in the sun-dried tomatoes. Spoon into a bowl and chill, covered, for 2 hours.

Beat the cream cheese and butter in a mixing bowl until creamy. Add the Parmesan cheese and pesto and beat until smooth; set aside. Line a 3-cup bowl or mold with plastic wrap, letting the sides hang over at least 6 inches. Cut 5 slices of the Muenster cheese in half diagonally and arrange in a spiral, slightly overlapping, around the inside of the bowl. Spread half of the cream cheese mixture over the cheese slices. Top with half of the tomato sauce mixture. Cut the remaining 4 slices of cheese in half horizontally and arrange 4 slices over the tomato sauce layer. Top with the remaining cream cheese mixture, remaining tomato sauce and remaining slices of cheese. Fold the plastic wrap over the top of the bowl and seal securely. Place a heavy object on top to compress the layers. Chill for at least 8 hours or up to 3 days.

Invert onto a serving plate to unmold, peeling off the plastic wrap. Cut out a wedge before serving so that the layers are visible. Serve with baguette slices.

Yield: 12 servings

Goat Cheese Marinara with Herb Toast

Sometimes the simplest of ingredients can create the most spectacular of treats.

1 (15-ounce) jar marinara sauce
1 (4-ounce) log goat cheese
1 loaf French bread, cut into
1/2-inch slices
2 tablespoons extra-virgin
olive oil

1/2 teaspoon garlic powder
1/2 teaspoon oregano
1/2 teaspoon basil
1/4 teaspoon salt
1/4 teaspoon pepper

Pour the marinara sauce into a decorative ovenproof baking dish. Place the goat cheese in the center; set aside. Place the bread slices in a large sealable plastic bag. Drizzle the olive oil over the bread slices. Sprinkle the garlic powder, oregano, basil, salt and pepper over the bread. Seal the bag and shake well to coat the bread slices with the olive oil and seasonings. Arrange the bread slices on a baking sheet. Bake at 400 degrees until brown and crispy. Increase the oven temperature to broil. Broil the cheese and marinara until the cheese is slightly blackened and marinara is bubbly. Serve with the toast.

Yield: 8 servings

Blue Cashew Spread

A member who now lives in the Grand Cayman Islands says she has been serving this spread for 42 years. It has surely stood the test of time. This can easily be made ahead and frozen.

1 (8- to 10-ounce) wedge
bleu cheese

3 ounces cream cheese, softened
1/2 cup finely chopped cashews

Mix the bleu cheese and cream cheese in a bowl until well blended. Add 2 teaspoons of the cashews and mix well. Shape the cheese mixture into a ball or a log. Roll in the remaining cashews until the cheese is well coated. Chill until firm. Serve on a plate with assorted crackers.

Yield: 8 to 10 servings

SASSY SALSA

This is a great appetizer for any gathering. Serve with blue or red tortilla chips for even more color and flavor.

2 (15-ounce) cans black beans,
  drained, rinsed
1 (16-ounce) can corn, drained
1/2 cup chopped fresh cilantro
1/4 cup chopped green onions
1/4 cup chopped red onion
1/3 cup fresh lime juice
3 tablespoons vegetable oil

1 tablespoon cumin
Salt to taste
Freshly ground pepper to taste
1 cup chopped tomatoes
1 cup chopped avocado
1 (4-ounce) can green chiles
  (optional)
Hot sauce (optional)

Combine the beans, corn, cilantro, green onions, red onion, lime juice, oil and cumin in a large bowl and mix well. Add the salt and pepper. Chill, covered, for up to 24 hours. Stir in the tomatoes, avocado and green chiles immediately before serving. You may also add hot sauce to taste if desired. Serve with corn chips or crostini.

Yield: 6 cups (12 to 15 servings)

CENTERPIECE TIPS

The decorative elements of your table help set the mood for your gathering.

A pitcher full of daisies can have as much impact as a professional

arrangement. Fresh flowers are only one option for a centerpiece.

Try these ideas at your next party: Statues; fruit mounded high in a beautiful

bowl or stacked on a cake plate; vegetables mixed with flowers and fruit;

dried flowers; flowers and candles floating in shallow glass bowls

filled with water. Scatter small arrangements throughout a buffet or

line them down the center of the table.

GAZPACHO BLANCO

Pour into a thermos, pack the garnishes, and head for a picnic with this
creamy variation of the cold Spanish soup.

3 to 4 cucumbers, peeled, chopped
1 garlic clove
3 cups chicken broth
2 cups sour cream or low-fat sour cream
1 cup plain yogurt
3 tablespoons white vinegar

2 teaspoons salt
1/4 teaspoon pepper
4 tomatoes, peeled, chopped
1/2 cup chopped green onions
1/2 cup chopped fresh parsley
1/2 cup chopped green bell pepper
1/2 cup (or more) croutons

Process the cucumbers and garlic in a blender or food processor with a small amount of the chicken broth until well mixed. Add the remaining chicken broth and process until puréed.

Combine the sour cream and yogurt in a large bowl. Add the puréed cucumber mixture gradually, stirring until thin and well blended. Stir in the vinegar, salt and pepper. Chill, covered, for at least 6 hours. Serve the tomatoes, green onions, parsley, bell pepper and croutons in separate bowls as garnishes. Serve the gazpacho in chilled bowls as a first course.

Yield: 6 to 12 servings

CENTERPIECE TIPS

Use individual vases or pots of flowers at each place setting.

Almost anything around your house will serve as a unique container;

look in your own backyard for greenery—even sprigs off a bush or

magnolia blossoms make a beautiful presentation. Remember to

keep arrangements low on a table where guests will be seated so

they don't have to crane their necks to see each other.

BUNCO JUMBLE

People love this! Is it candy or a salty snack? You can be as creative as you want and use mini cookies, graham cracker bears, popcorn, candy corn, or pecans. It also makes a great party favor when wrapped in a plastic bag and tied with bright-colored raffia.

1 box mini Ritz peanut butter
sandwich crackers
1 cup dry roasted peanuts
1 (12-ounce) bag mini pretzel
sticks or twists
1 cup sugar
1/2 cup (1 stick) butter

1/2 cup light corn syrup
2 tablespoons vanilla extract
1 teaspoon baking soda
1 (10-ounce) package mini or
regular "M&M's" chocolate
candies

Combine the sandwich crackers, peanuts and pretzels in a large roasting pan. Heat the sugar, butter and corn syrup in a saucepan over medium-high heat. Bring to a boil and cook for 5 minutes, stirring frequently. Stir in the vanilla and baking soda. Pour over the cracker mixture, stirring to coat well. Bake at 250 degrees for 45 minutes, stirring the mixture every 15 minutes. Remove to waxed paper to let cool completely. Add the chocolate candies. Break up the mixture into small pieces as necessary.

Yield: handfuls of fun

PARTY FAVORS

Remember goody bags? Everybody loves to leave the party with

a little something. Remember, a party favor should be something small,

a remembrance of the evening, not something elaborate that makes

your guests feel obliged to reciprocate. Plant one of the herbs used in one of

your recipes in a small clay pot and tie with a pretty ribbon. Make a CD

of the music played during the party and give copies to your guests.

HOT AND SPICY SPINACH DIP

*A guaranteed crowd pleaser, this would be a sure starter at a casual
evening party or before the big game.*

1/2 onion, finely chopped
1/2 cup (1 stick) butter
2 (10-ounce) packages frozen
   chopped spinach,
   thawed, drained
8 ounces cream cheese,
   cut into cubes
1 cup sour cream
3/4 cup grated Parmesan cheese

1 (14-ounce) can artichoke
   hearts, drained, chopped
Crushed red pepper flakes
   to taste
Salt to taste
Pepper to taste
1 cup shredded Pepper
   Jack cheese

Sauté the onion in the butter in a large skillet until tender. Add the spinach, cream cheese, sour cream and Parmesan cheese, mixing well after each addition. Stir in the artichoke hearts, red pepper flakes, salt and pepper; remove from the heat. Pour into a baking dish. Top with the Pepper Jack cheese. Bake at 350 degrees for 30 minutes or until bubbly. You may also microwave on High for 4 to 5 minutes or until bubbly. Serve hot with assorted crackers and bread slices.

Yield: 12 servings

PARTY FAVORS

*Put place cards in pretty little frames and let your guests take them
home. Take-home bags of cookies or candied nuts are a nice way
to end the evening as well as flavored vinegar or oil in a beautiful glass jar,
a small beribboned box with a yummy chocolate, or a handwritten
recipe card of one of the evening's dishes.*

HOT SWISS BACON DIP

Our recipe tasters couldn't get enough of this unusual dip. You may prepare this ahead of time and refrigerate. Bring to room temperature and bake just before serving time.

8 ounces cream cheese, softened
1/2 cup mayonnaise
1 cup shredded Swiss cheese
2 tablespoons finely chopped
green onions

8 slices bacon, crisp-cooked,
crumbled
1 sleeve butter crackers, crushed
3 tablespoons melted butter

Combine the cream cheese, mayonnaise and Swiss cheese in a bowl and mix well. Stir in the green onions and bacon. Spread into a shallow baking dish. Top with the crushed crackers and drizzle with the melted butter. Bake at 350 degrees for 20 to 25 minutes. Serve hot with assorted crackers or chips.

Yield: 8 to 12 servings

WARM CRAB DIP

Inspired by time spent by a member in Annapolis, Maryland, this recipe is always a buffet favorite. It can be easily doubled and served in a beautiful chafing dish.

8 ounces cream cheese,
cut into cubes
3 tablespoons mayonnaise
2 tablespoons prepared
horseradish

1/2 teaspoon salt
1/4 teaspoon pepper
8 ounces back-fin or lump crab
meat, flaked
2 tablespoons white wine

Combine the cream cheese, mayonnaise, horseradish, salt and pepper in a double boiler. Cook until the cream cheese is melted and the mixture is heated through, stirring frequently. Stir in the crab meat and wine immediately before serving. Serve warm with assorted crackers and French bread slices. You may spoon into a chafing dish to keep warm while serving.

Yield: 6 to 8 servings

APPLETINI

This version of the martini is the color of Granny Smith apples. This would be an unexpected treat at a spring get-together.

2 ounces apple schnapps
2 ounces premium vodka
Splash of applejack
Crushed ice

Combine the apple schnapps, vodka, applejack and ice in a cocktail shaker; cover. Shake vigorously and strain into chilled martini glasses.

Yield: 2 servings

CHIC COSMOPOLITANS

A refreshing and hip version of a vodka martini.

1 cup cranberry juice cocktail
6 tablespoons vodka
1/4 cup Grand Marnier
4 teaspoons fresh lemon juice
Crushed ice

Combine the cranberry juice, vodka, Grand Marnier, lemon juice and ice in a cocktail shaker; cover. Shake vigorously and strain into chilled martini glasses.

Yield: 2 servings

PEACH CHAMPAGNE COCKTAIL

Celebrations are always more festive when drinking Champagne, and we think this one is even more special with its beautiful golden color.

1 tablespoon peach schnapps
1 teaspoon amaretto
Champagne, chilled

Pour the peach schnapps and amaretto into a Champagne flute. Top with chilled Champagne. Serve immediately.

Yield: 1 serving

CHAMPAGNE 101

There are three main varieties of Champagne: Brut, Extra-Dry, and Rosé. Brut is the driest, crisp and medium-bodied. Extra-Dry has a touch of sugar added and works well with fresh fruit. Rosé is made with the addition of red wine, giving it a salmon-pink hue. It is the fullest of the three.

MOJITO

The classic Cuban cocktail that melds the flavors of rum, mint, and lime.
Warning, it is hard to drink just one!

16 mint leaves	6 tablespoons white rum
3 tablespoons sugar	Crushed ice
2 tablespoons fresh lime juice	1 cup club soda

Crush the mint leaves, sugar and lime juice in a small glass with the back of a spoon. Add the rum and mix until the sugar dissolves. Fill 2 wine glasses with ice. Strain the rum mixture through a sieve into the wine glasses, pressing on the mint leaves to extract all the juice. Top with the club soda and garnish with mint leaves or lime wedges.

Yield: 2 servings

GARDEN SANGRIA

This is almost too pretty to drink served in a clear pitcher with fruit floating throughout.
If you are serving it in a punch bowl, we recommend using an ice ring made of lemonade, which
flavors the sangria as it melts. To make it, pour lemonade into a ring mold and freeze.

1 large orange	1 cup Triple Sec or Grand
1 lemon	Marnier
1 lime	2 bottles dry white wine, chilled
2 or 3 cinnamon sticks	1/2 cup sugar
1 cup vodka	1 quart club soda, chilled

Thinly slice the orange, lemon and lime; remove all seeds. Place the fruit slices in a bowl with the cinnamon sticks. Pour the vodka and Triple Sec over the fruit slices. Chill, covered, for 4 to 12 hours.

Combine the chilled wine and sugar in a large glass pitcher or punch bowl. Pour the fruit mixture into the pitcher, discarding the cinnamon sticks. Add the club soda. Stir well before serving. Whole star anise make an attractive garnish if desired.

Yield: 20 servings

WINE PUNCH

*Looking for a different drink to serve at your party? Try this sangria-like punch, which
would be a hit at Bunco or a book club gathering.*

4 cups Burgundy wine
4 cups blush wine
2 cups chilled orange juice
1 (2-liter) bottle chilled lemon-lime soda
1 (12-ounce) can frozen pink lemonade concentrate, thawed

Combine the Burgundy wine, blush wine, orange juice, soda and lemonade concentrate in a large
container; mix well. Chill until serving time. Pour into a punch bowl to serve.

Yield: 15 to 20 servings

CITRUS SLUSH

*This reminded us of a frozen gin and tonic. Move over spring; summer is
here with this light and tangy drink.*

1 (6-ounce) can frozen limeade concentrate, thawed
6 ounces gin
1 quart citrus soft drink
2 drops green food coloring (optional)

Combine the limeade concentrate, gin, soft drink and food coloring in a large container. Freeze
until serving time. Thaw until slushy and serve in a punch bowl.

Yield: 20 servings

PIRATE'S MILK PUNCH

We have known many a pirate who has enjoyed this beverage before the Gasparilla invasion. Now we can all enjoy this brunch classic. Pour into silver julep cups, sprinkle freshly grated nutmeg on top, and await the accolades.

1 cup sugar	1 cup high-quality vodka
1 cup high-quality bourbon (do not use sour mash bourbon)	2 ounces pure vanilla extract (do not use imitation vanilla)
1 cup French brandy (such as Cognac)	1 teaspoon freshly grated nutmeg
	Whole milk

Combine the sugar, bourbon, brandy and vodka in a gallon container with a lid. An empty gallon milk jug will work. Secure the lid and shake vigorously until the sugar is dissolved. Add the vanilla and nutmeg; shake well. Add the milk, 2 cups at a time, until the jug is full; shaking well after each addition. Chill for 8 to 24 hours before serving. Serve very cold or over ice in old-fashioned glasses. Sprinkle freshly grated nutmeg over the top before serving.

Yield: 1 gallon (16 servings)

MOCHACCINO PUNCH

We served this at our first tasting event and were immediately inundated with requests for the recipe. It is a great choice for a morning coffee or brunch.

1/4 cup instant coffee granules	1 1/2 teaspoons vanilla extract
1 cup sugar	1/3 cup chocolate syrup
6 cups hot water	1/2 gallon vanilla ice cream, softened
1 quart whole milk	

Combine the coffee granules, sugar and hot water in a punch bowl. Stir until the granules and sugar are dissolved; let cool. Add the milk, vanilla and chocolate syrup; mix well. Chill for 2 hours or until ready to serve. Add the ice cream immediately before serving. Ladle into punch cups to serve.

Yield: 14 to 16 generous servings

THE LIFE OF THE PARTY

SIDELINERS

CULINARY COLLECTION

LINGUINE AL GRANCHIO CON SALSA ROSA (LINGUINE WITH CRAB IN A PINK SAUCE)

Chef Paolo Tini of Caffé Paradiso shared this signature dish from his award-winning restaurant. The pink sauce is just the right touch for the tender crab.

1/2 onion, chopped	3 ounces olive oil
3 ounces olive oil	1 pound lump crab meat, flaked
1 (9-ounce) can Italian plum	1 cup clam juice
tomatoes, puréed	1 cup heavy cream
Salt to taste	1 pound linguine or angel hair
Pepper to taste	pasta, cooked
2 tablespoons minced garlic	

Sauté the onion in 3 ounces olive oil in a skillet until tender. Add the puréed tomatoes, salt and pepper. Reduce the heat and simmer for 30 minutes.

Sauté the garlic in 3 ounces olive oil in a separate skillet until tender and golden. Add the crab meat and clam juice. Simmer for 2 minutes. Reduce the heat and stir in the tomato sauce and heavy cream. Simmer for 10 minutes. Serve over the hot cooked linguine. Garnish with ribbons of fresh basil.

Yield: 4 to 6 servings

SELECTING WINE

When selecting a wine, always think of what you are planning to serve to eat. Try to find professionals you trust and ask their opinions. Tell them clearly what your preferences are and give them a price to work with. Most of all, don't be afraid to try new things.

ARTICHOKE AND ORZO SALAD

A creamy, rich side dish for grilled or roasted meats and poultry.

1¹/2 cups orzo
¹/4 cup olive oil
1 egg yolk
2 tablespoons white wine vinegar
1 teaspoon Dijon mustard
Salt to taste
Pepper to taste
¹/2 cup olive oil
2 tablespoons finely chopped fresh basil
2 ounces finely chopped prosciutto
2 ounces Parmesan cheese, grated
2 tablespoons (or more) fresh lemon juice
¹/4 cup finely chopped fresh parsley
4 scallions, finely chopped
1 (9-ounce) package frozen artichoke hearts, thawed

Cook the orzo in boiling water in a large saucepan for 8 minutes or until al dente; drain. Toss the orzo in a large bowl with ¹/4 cup olive oil; set aside.

Whisk the egg yolk in a bowl with the white wine vinegar, Dijon mustard, salt and pepper. Whisk in ¹/2 cup olive oil in a fine stream. Mix in the basil and pour over the orzo, tossing to coat well.

Add the prosciutto, Parmesan cheese, lemon juice, parsley and scallions and mix well. Fold in the artichokes. Season with additional salt and pepper if necessary. Garnish with fresh basil leaves if desired. You may substitute canned artichoke hearts for the frozen.

Note: You may use an equivalent amount of pasteurized egg substitute to avoid raw eggs.

Yield: 4 servings

BLACK BEAN AND JASMINE RICE SALAD

An innovative combination of the traditional black beans and rice with a salad.

2 cups cooked black beans
2 cups cooked jasmine rice
1 cup olive oil
1/4 cup Key lime juice
2 garlic cloves, minced
Salt to taste

Freshly ground pepper to taste
1/2 cup chopped scallions
 (optional)
2 tablespoons chopped fresh
 cilantro (optional)
1/2 to 1 head romaine

Combine the beans and rice in a large bowl. Whisk the olive oil into the lime juice in a small bowl. Add the garlic, salt and pepper. Pour over the beans and rice, tossing to coat well. Stir in the scallions and cilantro. Chill, covered, until serving time. Cut or tear the romaine into bite-size pieces. Fold into the salad immediately before serving.

You may substitute 2 (15-ounce) cans of black beans for the cooked black beans. Rinse and drain the canned beans before preparing the salad.

For extra flavor, reduce some balsamic vinegar until it is of a syrupy consistency. Let it cool and drizzle over the salad before serving.

Yield: 8 to 10 servings

GUEST LIST

The most important ingredient you will add to your gathering

is the guest list. Try to select a blend of guests, those who can get

the conversation started and those who love to listen. When

seating guests at a sit-down dinner, make sure the conversationalists

are scattered around the table.

GOAT CHEESE TABBOULEH WITH LEMON VINAIGRETTE

A twist on the Middle Eastern specialty. Serve in hollowed-out cherry tomatoes for a pick-up snack or with a sandwich for a great do-ahead side salad.

4 cups water
1/2 teaspoon salt
2 ears fresh corn
1 cup bulgur wheat
1/2 red onion, finely chopped
1 large tomato, chopped
1/2 cup finely chopped celery
1/4 cup finely chopped scallions
1/4 cup extra-virgin olive oil
1/3 cup fresh lemon juice
1 cup chopped fresh cilantro
4 ounces goat cheese, crumbled
Salt to taste
Freshly ground pepper to taste

Bring the water to a boil with the salt in a saucepan. Shave the kernels from the ears of corn into the boiling water. Boil for 2 to 3 minutes. Strain the water from the corn into a large bowl, reserving the corn in a separate bowl. Add the bulgur wheat to the hot corn water. Let stand for 20 minutes or until tender. Drain any excess water from the bulgur wheat.

Combine the corn, bulgur wheat, onion, tomato, celery and scallions in a large bowl. Mix in the olive oil and lemon juice. Fold in the cilantro and goat cheese. Season with salt and pepper. You may serve warm or cold.

Yield: 4 servings

GUACAMOLE SALAD

Submitted by Chef Jeannie Pierola, Chef/Partner at SideBern's Restaurant and Executive Chef/Culinary Director at Bern's Steak House. The smooth-as-silk avocados, crunchy peppers, and onions make this a perfect complement to barbeque. You might find yourself eating this straight out of the bowl!

4 avocados, cubed	Juice of 2 limes
2 red bell peppers, chopped	1/4 cup extra-virgin olive oil
2 yellow bell peppers, chopped	2 pinches ground cumin
1 red onion, chopped	Kosher salt to taste
1/2 cup chopped fresh cilantro	Freshly ground pepper to taste

Combine the avocados, bell peppers, onion and cilantro in a large bowl. Add the lime juice, olive oil, cumin, salt and pepper and toss to coat well. Chill, covered, until serving time.

Yield: 8 servings

THE MENU

When selecting the menu, consider the occasion. Is this the time to try something new (buffets are great for this) or to stick with what you know? Plan your menu, check your pantry, and make your shopping list. Do as much cooking as you can in advance of the party so on that day you are able to add the final touches and focus on your guests. Enlist the help of a close friend or professional to assist in the preparation if needed.

ASIAN SLAW

Coleslaw is an ever-popular salad. We think this one is a great change of pace with oriental flavors, bright colors, and a variety of textures. Garnish with fresh cilantro and chopped peanuts.

DRESSING
3 tablespoons rice wine vinegar
1 tablespoon Dijon mustard
3/4 cup safflower or peanut oil
2 tablespoons soy sauce
1 tablespoon honey
1 teaspoon sesame oil
2 garlic cloves, minced
2 teaspoons minced fresh gingerroot
Salt to taste
Pepper to taste

SALAD
4 cups chopped green cabbage
4 cups chopped red cabbage
1 carrot, grated
4 scallions, sliced
1/4 cup dry roasted peanuts, chopped
3 tablespoons chopped fresh cilantro

For the dressing, mix the rice wine vinegar and Dijon mustard in a bowl with a whisk. Add the safflower oil in a fine stream, whisking until well blended. Add the soy sauce, honey, sesame oil, garlic, gingerroot, salt and pepper and mix well.

For the salad, combine the green cabbage, red cabbage, carrot, scallions, peanuts and cilantro in a large bowl. Add the dressing to the salad and toss to coat well. Chill, covered, until serving time.

Yield: 6 to 8 servings

MARINATED TOMATOES

Fresh, ripe tomatoes are essential for this recipe. The simple ingredients highlight the flavor of the tomatoes without overpowering them.

3 large tomatoes, cut into 1/2-inch-thick slices
1/2 cup olive oil
1/4 cup red wine vinegar
2 tablespoons minced onion
2 tablespoons (or more) chopped
fresh basil
1 tablespoon chopped fresh parsley
1/2 garlic clove, minced
1 teaspoon salt
1/4 teaspoon pepper

Arrange the tomatoes in a shallow dish; set aside. Combine the olive oil, red wine vinegar, onion, basil, parsley, garlic, salt and pepper in a jar with a tight-fitting lid. Secure the lid and shake vigorously to mix well. Pour over the tomato slices. Marinate, covered, in the refrigerator for up to 24 hours. Serve with a slotted spoon.

You may substitute 2 teaspoons dried basil for the fresh basil.

Yield: 6 to 8 servings

SWEET AND SALTY TOMATO SALAD

This recipe was inspired by an article in a French magazine. The unusual combination of tomatoes and cantaloupe creates a memorable accompaniment.

2 pints cherry or grape tomatoes
1 cantaloupe
1/2 cup crumbled feta cheese
1 bunch arugula, torn
Zest of 1 lemon
1/4 cup olive oil

2 tablespoons balsamic vinegar,
    or juice of 1 lemon
1 bunch fresh basil, chopped
Salt to taste
Pepper to taste

Cut the tomatoes into halves and place in a large salad bowl. Cut the cantaloupe into balls with a melon baller and add to the tomatoes. Add the feta cheese, arugula and lemon zest; mix well.

Combine the olive oil, balsamic vinegar, basil, salt and pepper in a small bowl and whisk to mix well. Pour over the salad immediately before serving. Toss to coat well.

Variation: For Corn, Tomato and Arugula Salad, substitute corn kernels and bleu cheese for the melon balls and feta cheese. Add 1/2 cup chopped red onion and omit the basil.

Yield: 8 servings

PARTY HELP

Consider renting if you do not have all the necessary gear

or just want a new look. From glasses to tables, just about anything

you need for a party can be rented. Also consider hiring help to

assist in serving, cleaning up, or tending bar.

MANDARIN SALAD WITH PEANUT DRESSING

For nights when you want a different salad, perhaps with a little Asian influence.
This would make a nice complement to a grilled pork tenderloin.

PEANUT DRESSING

6 tablespoons water	1 garlic clove
3 tablespoons sherry	1 tablespoon chopped fresh
2 tablespoons light soy sauce	gingerroot
1 tablespoon red wine vinegar	6 tablespoons peanut butter
1 tablespoon brown sugar	1/2 cup vegetable or peanut oil

SALAD AND WON TON STRIPS

1 large bunch romaine, torn	2 oranges, sectioned
into bite-size pieces	1/2 package won ton wrappers,
4 to 5 scallions, green tips only,	cut into thin strips
thinly sliced	(optional)
1/2 cup cashew halves	

For the dressing, combine the water, sherry, soy sauce, red wine vinegar, brown sugar, garlic, gingerroot and peanut butter in a blender. Process until smooth. Add the oil in a fine stream, pulsing until well blended.

For the salad, combine the romaine, scallions, cashews and orange sections in a large salad bowl. Chill, covered, until serving time.

For the won ton strips, heat vegetable or peanut oil in a skillet until hot. Fry the won ton strips until golden and crispy. Remove with a slotted spoon to paper towels to drain.

To serve, sprinkle the salad with the won ton strips. Pour the dressing over the salad and toss to coat well. Serve immediately.

Note: To section an orange, cut the top off a navel orange with a sharp knife. Remove the peel from top to bottom, using a knife disturbing as little of the orange pulp as possible. Continue around the orange until all the peel is removed. Cut sections out between the membranes.

Yield: 6 servings

FESTIVAL STRAWBERRY SALAD

One of our members and a cookbook author, Laura York, submitted this delicious salad highlighting one of our locally grown specialties, strawberries. She was awarded the 1989 Grand Championship at the Florida Strawberry Festival for this tasty salad.

SWEET-AND-SOUR DRESSING
1/2 cup vegetable oil
1/4 cup vinegar
2 tablespoons sugar
10 drops of red pepper sauce
1 teaspoon salt
Dash of black pepper

SALAD
1 head romaine, torn into bite-size pieces
2 ribs celery, chopped
2 1/2 cups strawberries, sliced
1 (11-ounce) can mandarin oranges, drained

GLAZED ALMONDS
1/4 cup sliced almonds
1 tablespoon plus 1 teaspoon sugar

For the dressing, combine the oil, vinegar, sugar, red pepper sauce, salt and pepper in a jar with a tight-fitting lid. Secure the lid and shake vigorously to mix well.

For the salad, combine the romaine, celery, strawberries and mandarin oranges in a large salad bowl.

For the almonds, combine the almonds and sugar in a small skillet over low heat, stirring constantly until sugar is dissolved and the almonds are well coated. Pour onto waxed paper to cool. Break the almonds into small pieces.

To serve, pour the dressing over the salad and toss to combine. Sprinkle the almonds over the top and serve immediately.

Yield: 4 to 6 servings

LAYERED SPINACH SALAD

For entertaining, a layered salad is a dream come true. It is prepared ahead of time,
beautiful in presentation, and always a hit. Let your imagination be your guide
in creating new combinations for your next party.

DRESSING
1 cup mayonnaise
1/2 cup sour cream
2 tablespoons minced red onion
2 tablespoons water
2 teaspoons cider vinegar
2 teaspoons prepared horseradish
2 teaspoons sugar
1/2 teaspoon salt
1/2 teaspoon pepper

SALAD
12 ounces fresh baby spinach leaves
1 red bell pepper, chopped
1 yellow bell pepper, chopped
6 ounces fresh mushrooms, sliced
1 pint cherry or grape tomatoes, halved
1 cup frozen tiny peas, thawed
4 hard-cooked eggs, sliced
6 slices bacon, crisp-cooked, crumbled

For the dressing, combine the mayonnaise, sour cream, onion, water, cider vinegar, horseradish, sugar, salt and pepper in a bowl; mix until smooth.

For the salad, layer the spinach, bell peppers, mushrooms, tomatoes, peas and eggs in a large clear glass bowl. Spoon the dressing evenly over the top. Chill, covered, for at least 2 hours before serving. Sprinkle the bacon over the top immediately before serving. Spoon through all layers to serve. You may substitute light sour cream and light mayonnaise in the dressing if desired.

Yield: 8 to 10 servings

SALAD DRESSING TO-DIE-FOR

Yes, this is true. This dressing has a great blend of flavors and is an all-purpose dressing for almost any salad.

1 cup vegetable oil
3/4 cup cider vinegar
1/3 cup sugar
1 tablespoon salt
4 garlic cloves, minced

Combine the oil, cider vinegar, sugar, salt and garlic in a blender. Process on high speed until well blended and smooth. Pour into an airtight container with a tight-fitting lid. Shake vigorously before serving. Store in the refrigerator.

Yield: 2 cups

MAPLE RASPBERRY VINAIGRETTE

A slightly sweet dressing that is terrific on field greens, gorgonzola, onion, and pine nuts. Also delicious over spinach and bacon salads.

1/4 cup raspberry vinegar
1/4 cup maple syrup
1 tablespoon tarragon
2 teaspoons Dijon mustard
Salt to taste
Freshly ground pepper to taste
1 cup (about) canola oil

Mix the raspberry vinegar, syrup, tarragon, Dijon mustard, salt and pepper in a bowl. Whisk in the canola oil in a fine stream until well blended and of the desired consistency. Store in the refrigerator.

Yield: 1 1/2 cups

ASPARAGUS PECAN STACK

Nothing says spring like fresh asparagus. Look for thin, freshly cut spears for the best straight-out-of-the-garden taste.

1¹/2 pounds fresh asparagus
³/4 cup finely chopped pecans
2 tablespoons vegetable oil
¹/4 cup cider vinegar

¹/4 cup soy sauce
¹/4 cup sugar
Freshly ground pepper to taste

Steam the asparagus in 1 to 2 inches of boiling water for 6 to 7 minutes or until bright green. Rinse under cold water and drain. Layer the asparagus and pecans in an oblong serving dish. Whisk the oil, cider vinegar, soy sauce and sugar in a bowl until well blended. Pour evenly over the asparagus. Season with pepper. Marinate, in the refrigerator, for 2 to 3 hours. May be prepared a couple days in advance.

Yield: 4 to 6 servings

PESTO GREEN BEANS

Looking for new ways to serve vegetables? The herbs and nuts of the pesto are just right with the crispy green beans.

¹/2 cup packed fresh basil leaves
2 tablespoons chopped pecans,
    toasted
2 tablespoons olive oil
1 garlic clove
1¹/2 tablespoons lemon juice

¹/2 teaspoon salt
1 pound fresh green beans,
    trimmed
2 tablespoons chopped pecans,
    toasted

Process the basil, 2 tablespoons pecans, olive oil, garlic, lemon juice and salt in a blender until smooth. Steam the green beans for 10 to 12 minutes or until tender-crisp. Pour the pesto over the hot green beans in a serving bowl, tossing to coat well. Sprinkle with 2 tablespoons pecans. Serve immediately.

Yield: 4 to 6 servings

CHUTNEY CARROTS

Chutney proves to be the perfect condiment to bring out the sweetness of carrots.
Top with fresh herbs for an aromatic garnish.

8 slices bacon
1 onion, chopped
1/2 cup sugar
1/2 cup vinegar
1 bunch carrots, peeled, thinly sliced
3 tablespoons prepared chutney

Cook the bacon in a skillet until tender-crisp. Remove the bacon to paper towels to drain; reserve the drippings. Crumble the bacon.

Sauté the onion in the bacon drippings. Add the sugar and vinegar and cook until the sugar is dissolved. Spoon the carrots into a baking dish. Pour the onion mixture over the carrots. Combine the chutney and crumbled bacon in a small bowl. Spoon over the top of the carrots. Bake at 275 degrees for 1 hour and 30 minutes.

Yield: 6 to 8 servings

CORN SOUFFLÉ

This is a warm and comforting accompaniment to barbequed and grilled meats. Add shredded
cheese, chopped green chiles, or chipotle peppers for a variation.

1 (15-ounce) can cream-style corn
1 (15-ounce) can whole kernel corn, drained
1/2 cup (1 stick) butter, melted
2 eggs, beaten
1 cup sour cream
1 package corn muffin mix

Combine the cream-style corn, whole kernel corn, melted butter, eggs, sour cream and corn muffin mix in a large bowl. Mix just until blended. Pour into a buttered baking dish. Bake at 350 degrees for 35 to 45 minutes.

Yield: 6 servings

CORN ROASTED IN ROMAINE

The creative use of romaine leaves in this recipe allows the herbs and butter to infuse the fresh corn with delicious flavors. These bundles can also be wrapped in foil and grilled.

1/4 cup (1/2 stick) butter, softened
1 teaspoon rosemary

1/2 teaspoon marjoram
6 ears of corn
1 head romaine

Mix the butter, rosemary and marjoram in a small bowl; spread some of the butter mixture on the corn. Wrap each ear of corn in 2 to 3 romaine leaves. Arrange in a shallow baking dish and cover tightly with foil. Bake at 450 degrees for 20 to 25 minutes. Discard the romaine leaves and serve the corn with the remaining butter.

Yield: 6 servings

PAPAS CON MOJO

Jeannie Pierola, Chef/Partner at SideBern's Restaurant and Executive Chef/Culinary Director at Bern's Steak House, does her magic with potatoes and mojo, a spicy Cuban specialty.

1 pound Yukon gold potatoes, cubed
Olive oil to coat
1 onion, sliced
1 tablespoon extra-virgin olive oil
1 garlic clove, minced

1/4 cup white wine
Juice of 6 oranges
1/2 bunch fresh cilantro, chopped
1/2 bunch fresh oregano, chopped
Kosher salt to taste
Freshly ground pepper to taste

Toss the potatoes with olive oil to coat in a large roasting pan. Roast the potatoes at 400 degrees until golden brown, stirring once. Sauté the onion in 1 tablespoon olive oil in a skillet until tender. Add the garlic and sauté for 2 minutes. Spoon the onion and garlic into a bowl. Deglaze the sauté pan with the white wine and reduce until the liquid is almost gone. Add the orange juice and reduce by about 2/3. Pour the liquid over the onion mixture. Fold in the cilantro and oregano. Season with salt and pepper. Pour the hot mojo sauce over the roasted potatoes. Serve immediately.

Yield: 8 servings

WHITE TRUFFLE MASHED POTATOES

This version of the ultimate comfort food is flavored with white truffle oil. It imparts an earthy mushroom flavor that sets it apart from your standard mashed potatoes.

2 pounds Yukon gold potatoes, peeled, cubed
1 cup milk or half-and-half
3 tablespoons butter
Salt to taste
Pepper to taste
3 tablespoons white truffle oil

Cook the potatoes in salted boiling water in a saucepan until tender and easily pierced with a fork; drain. Spoon into a large mixing bowl. Add the milk and butter. Beat until very smooth. You may add more milk if necessary for the desired consistency. Season with salt and pepper. Fold in the truffle oil. Serve immediately.

To prepare in advance, spoon into a baking dish and let cool. Chill, covered, until ready to bake. Add a small amount of additional milk. Bake at 350 degrees for 30 minutes or until heated through.

White truffle oil is available at specialty food stores. Refrigerate after opening.

Yield: 8 servings

PARTY DIARY

Keep a party diary. List the occasion and who was invited.

Keep a copy of the invitation if there was one and record what was

served. Be sure to note what worked and what didn't. Don't forget

to record what you gave as the party favor. Take pictures of your

tables and food before guests arrive. Refer to your diary

when planning future events.

GORGONZOLA SOUFFLÉS

Chef Rob Stanford of the Tampa Yacht & Country Club submitted this light and flavorful soufflé that pairs well with a tenderloin or roasted chicken.

5 tablespoons butter
1/2 cup flour
2 cups milk
8 ounces gorgonzola cheese, crumbled
1 tablespoon Dijon mustard
5 egg yolks
4 ounces gorgonzola cheese, crumbled
6 egg whites
Juice of 1/2 lemon

Melt the butter in a saucepan. Stir in the flour and cook for 1 minute. Whisk in the milk until well blended and thickened. Simmer for 30 seconds. Whisk in 8 ounces gorgonzola cheese and the Dijon mustard. Cook until the cheese is melted. Remove from the heat and cool. Whisk in the egg yolks. Stir in 4 ounces gorgonzola cheese.

Beat the egg whites and lemon juice in a mixing bowl until soft peaks form. Whisk 1/3 of the egg whites into the cheese sauce and fold in the remaining 2/3 of the egg whites.

Attach foil collars to 4 ramekins that extend 3 inches above the rims. Spray the inside with nonstick cooking spray. Pour the filling into the molds, filling them 1 inch above the rim. You may also bake in a large soufflé dish.

Bake at 400 degrees for 15 minutes or until well risen and set in the center. Remove to a wire rack and let cool. Soufflés will fall to about the original fill line, 1 inch above the rim. Remove the foil collars. Serve immediately or reheat slightly at serving time. If baking in a soufflé dish, increase baking time to 30 minutes or until well risen and set in the center.

Yield: 1 (8-cup) soufflé dish or 4 (4-ounce) ramekins

JALAPEÑO CHEESE GRITS

Traditional southern fare with a kick. Try this at a New Year's brunch or a tailgate.

7 cups water	1 cup (2 sticks) butter, melted
2 teaspoons salt	1/2 cup milk
2 cups stone-ground grits	4 eggs, beaten
1 (8-ounce) roll processed garlic cheese	Salt to taste
	Pepper to taste
8 ounces processed jalapeño cheese	

Combine the water and salt in a large saucepan; bring to a boil. Stir in the grits. Cook, covered, on low for 25 minutes. Cut the garlic cheese and jalapeño cheese into small pieces. Stir into the grits until melted; remove from the heat. Add the butter, milk, eggs, salt and pepper and mix well. Pour into a greased 9×13-inch baking dish. Bake at 350 degrees for 1 hour.

Yield: 12 servings

PIÑA COLADA MUFFINS

Using a cake mix as a base, these are quick to put together but complex in flavor. Prepare as mini muffins, pile into a linen-lined basket, and serve at your next brunch. Children love these as much as adults because they are almost as much fun as cupcakes!

1 (2-layer) package yellow cake mix	1 cup flaked coconut
	1 cup chopped nuts (preferably
1 teaspoon coconut extract	macadamia or pecans)
1 teaspoon rum flavoring	1 cup drained crushed pineapple

Prepare the cake mix according to the package directions. Stir in the coconut extract, rum flavoring, coconut, nuts and pineapple; do not overmix. Fill greased or paper-lined muffin cups 3/4 full. Bake at 350 degrees for 15 to 20 minutes or until a wooden pick inserted in the center comes out clean. You may also bake in mini muffin pans. Bake at 350 degrees for 12 minutes.

Yield: 30 regular muffins or 8 dozen mini muffins

LEMON POPPY SEED LOAF

Serve this sliced on a platter with strawberries and raspberries for a spring luncheon, or wrap it up and tie with ribbon for a great hostess gift.

BREAD
1/2 cup (1 stick) unsalted butter, softened
1 cup sugar
2 eggs
1 teaspoon lemon zest
1 1/2 cups flour
1 teaspoon baking powder
1/2 teaspoon salt
1/3 cup milk
2 tablespoons poppy seeds

GLAZE
3 tablespoons lemon juice
1 1/4 cups confectioners' sugar

For the bread, beat the butter and sugar in a mixing bowl until light and fluffy. Beat in the eggs, 1 at a time, mixing well after each addition. Add the lemon zest, flour, baking powder, salt and milk and beat at low speed until combined. Mix in the poppy seeds. Do not overmix the batter. Pour into a greased and floured 5×9-inch loaf pan. Bake at 350 degrees for 55 minutes or until a wooden pick inserted in the center comes out clean. Remove to a wire rack to cool.

For the glaze, combine the lemon juice and confectioners' sugar in a small bowl and mix well. Prick the top of the hot loaf with a fork. Pour the glaze slowly over the hot loaf. Wrap in plastic wrap and let stand for several hours to overnight before slicing to serve.

Yield: 12 servings

CINNAMON PULL

These breakfast rolls almost make themselves! There is nothing more inviting than the smell of freshly baked bread and cinnamon to make a guest feel at home.

1/2 package frozen dinner roll dough (use 12 to 18 rolls)
1/2 cup (1 stick) melted butter
1 (4-ounce) package vanilla cook-and-serve pudding
1/2 cup packed light brown sugar
1/2 cup chopped pecans
1 teaspoon cinnamon

Arrange the frozen rolls in a well-greased bundt pan, trying not to overlap rolls. Combine the melted butter, pudding mix, brown sugar, pecans and cinnamon in a small bowl; mix well. Pour evenly over the rolls. Cover with a clean kitchen towel. Let stand at room temperature for 8 hours or overnight to thaw and rise until doubled in bulk.

Bake at 350 degrees for 20 to 30 minutes. Let cool in the pan for a few minutes. Invert onto a serving plate. Pull apart rolls to serve.

Yield: 12 servings

PRALINE BRUNCH TOAST

You will love this dish for its marvelous flavors, and even more for the convenience of preparing it the night before. Weekend guests or visiting family will love waking up to this special treat.

8 eggs
1 1/2 cups half-and-half
1 tablespoon brown sugar
2 teaspoons vanilla extract
8 thick slices sourdough bread
1/2 cup (1 stick) butter
3/4 cup packed brown sugar
1/2 cup maple syrup
3/4 cup chopped pecans

Beat the eggs and half-and-half in a small bowl. Whisk in 1 tablespoon brown sugar and vanilla. Pour 1/2 of the egg mixture into a 9×13-inch baking dish. Arrange the bread slices in the dish, trimming crusts to fit if necessary. Pour the remaining egg mixture over the bread. Chill, covered, for several hours or overnight.

Melt the butter in another 9×13-inch baking dish. Stir in 3/4 cup brown sugar and the syrup. Sprinkle the pecans over the bottom. Place the egg-soaked bread slices carefully on top of the pecans with a spatula. Pour the remaining egg mixture over the bread. Bake at 350 degrees for 30 to 35 minutes or until the bread is light brown and puffed.

To serve, invert the toast onto plates and spoon pecans from the bottom of the dish over the toast.

Yield: 8 servings

BREAKFAST SORBET

This is a refreshing side dish for a brunch or luncheon. The cool texture is a great complement to savory, rich entrées.

1 (20-ounce) can crushed
   pineapple
1 (10-ounce) package frozen
   sliced strawberries, thawed
1 (10-ounce) package frozen
   raspberries, thawed

1 (6-ounce) can frozen orange
   juice concentrate, thawed
1 (6-ounce) can frozen pink
   lemonade concentrate,
   thawed
20 ounces ginger ale

Combine the pineapple, strawberries, raspberries, orange juice and lemonade in a large bowl; mix well. Stir in the ginger ale. Pour into a 9×13-inch dish. Freeze for 4 to 6 hours or until barely frozen and slushy. Spoon into festive margarita glasses or small fruit bowls to serve. Garnish with fresh mint sprigs, citrus zest or fresh berries if desired.

Yield: 10 to 12 servings

PINEAPPLE TEA

Garnish a tall tea glass with lemon and orange slices and long pineapple spears for stirring.

4 family-size tea bags
3 cups water
1 cup sugar
1 (46-ounce) can pineapple juice

2 1/4 cups orange juice
1/2 cup lemon juice
1 tablespoon almond extract
1 tablespoon vanilla extract

Prepare 3 cups very strong tea using the tea bags and water; pour into a gallon container. Stir in the sugar while the tea is hot; let cool. Add the pineapple juice, orange juice, lemon juice, almond extract and vanilla. Stir to mix well. Add enough cold water to fill the container.

Yield: 1 gallon (16 servings)

MAIN EVENTS

CHAMPAGNE SALMON PACKAGES

A wonderful choice for a do-ahead entrée that will have your guests asking, "How did you do that?"
This can be made into individual packets or one large package served in slices.

MOUSSE
6 ounces salmon
1 egg
Salt to taste
Pepper to taste
3/4 cup heavy cream

SALMON
2 sheets frozen puff pastry, thawed
1 (2-pound) salmon fillet
1 egg, beaten

CHAMPAGNE SAUCE
1/2 bottle Champagne
2 shallots, minced
3 cups heavy cream

For the mousse, place 6 ounces salmon in a food processor or blender. Process until smooth. Add the egg, salt and pepper. Add the cream slowly, processing until smooth. Spoon the mousse into a bowl. Chill, covered, for at least 1 hour.

For the salmon, roll out the pastry sheets on a work surface. Place the salmon fillet on 1 sheet and trim to fit. Butterfly the fillet lengthwise to create a pocket and flaps. Spoon the mousse into the pocket and press the flaps to close. Season with salt and pepper. Brush the edges of the pastry with some of the beaten egg. Place the other pastry sheet on top and press the edges to seal. Brush the entire top with the remaining beaten egg. Arrange the salmon on a baking sheet. Chill, covered, for at least 1 hour. You may cut shapes out of additional pastry to decorate the top if desired. Bake at 400 degrees for 20 minutes or until the pastry is golden brown.

For the sauce, combine the Champagne and shallots in a large saucepan and heat until reduced to a glaze. Add the cream and cook over medium heat until the sauce coats the back of a spoon. Season with salt and pepper. Cut the salmon into slices to serve. Spoon the sauce over the salmon immediately before serving.

Yield: 8 servings

GROUPER PROVENÇALE

Wrapping this fish in a foil package creates a moist and succulent entrée scented with herbs and citrus. This can easily be put on the grill or individually wrapped.

1 tablespoon olive oil	3 tablespoons white wine
3 pounds grouper fillets	5 tablespoons olive oil
Salt to taste	2 large tomatoes, sliced
Pepper to taste	1 large onion, sliced
2 tablespoons chopped	1 bay leaf, crushed
fresh parsley	Juice of 1 lemon
1/2 teaspoon thyme	

Line a baking sheet with foil and brush with 1 tablespoon olive oil. Arrange the fish in a single layer on the foil. Season with salt and pepper. Mix the parsley, thyme, wine and 5 tablespoons olive oil in a small bowl. Cover the fish with the tomato and onion slices. Pour the wine mixture over the top. Sprinkle with the crushed bay leaf and lemon juice. Cover with a sheet of foil, sealing the edges with the bottom foil layer. Bake at 350 degrees for 30 to 35 minutes or until the fish flakes easily. The grouper can also be prepared in individual packets of parchment paper.

Yield: 8 servings

WINE AND SEAFOOD

Sauce says everything when it comes to seafood. A light sauce,

such as a beurre blanc, is happiest with a citrusy Chardonnay, like a

Chablis. Heavy cream sauces want a light red. Morgon or

Moulin-a-Vent from Beaujolais partner well.

GRILLED SWORDFISH WITH CITRUS SALSA

The cool, tangy salsa is a fabulous accompaniment to the grilled fish. Although this recipe calls for swordfish, any firm fish will work.

CITRUS SALSA

3 oranges, peeled, white pith removed, seeded, chopped
1 1/2 cups chopped tomatoes
1/4 cup minced red onion
1/4 cup chopped fresh parsley
2 tablespoons fresh orange juice

2 teaspoons minced garlic
2 teaspoons balsamic vinegar
1/2 teaspoon grated fresh gingerroot
Salt to taste
Pepper to taste

MARINADE

3/4 cup teriyaki sauce
2/3 cup dry sherry
4 teaspoons minced garlic

1 1/2 teaspoons grated fresh gingerroot
1 teaspoon sesame oil

FISH

6 (5- to 6-ounce) 1-inch-thick swordfish steaks

For the salsa, combine the oranges, tomatoes, onion, parsley, orange juice, garlic, balsamic vinegar and gingerroot in a bowl and mix well. Season with salt and pepper. Let stand, covered, at room temperature for at least 30 minutes.

For the marinade, combine the teriyaki sauce, sherry, garlic, gingerroot and sesame oil in a saucepan. Bring to a boil; remove from the heat and let cool.

For the fish, arrange the swordfish steaks in a single layer in a shallow glass dish. Pour the marinade over the fish, turning to coat evenly. Marinate, covered, in the refrigerator for 1 hour, turning often. Remove the fish from the marinade; discard the marinade. Grill the fish over hot coals for 4 minutes on each side or until the fish flakes easily and is opaque in the center.

To serve, spoon a small amount of the salsa on each swordfish steak. Serve additional salsa on the side.

Yield: 6 servings

SHRIMP AND ORZO SALAD WITH BALSAMIC VINAIGRETTE

A light pasta salad for a baby shower or a celebration lunch. Combined with sliced fresh fruit, this will make a beautiful plate presentation.

BALSAMIC VINAIGRETTE

1 garlic clove, minced	1/2 cup olive oil
1 tablespoon brown sugar	Salt to taste
1 to 2 tablespoons Dijon mustard	Pepper to taste
1/2 cup white balsamic vinegar	

SALAD

2 bunches asparagus, trimmed	1 red bell pepper, chopped
6 cups water	1/2 cup finely chopped fresh basil
1 1/2 pounds unpeeled medium shrimp	2 tablespoons chopped fresh oregano
16 ounces orzo, cooked	6 cups gourmet salad greens
1 (14-ounce) can artichoke hearts, halved	Grated Parmesan cheese

For the vinaigrette, combine the garlic, brown sugar, Dijon mustard and balsamic vinegar in a blender. Process until blended, adding the olive oil in a fine stream. Season with salt and pepper. Store in an airtight container in the refrigerator until serving time.

For the salad, steam the asparagus, covered, for 8 minutes or until tender-crisp. Plunge the asparagus into cold water in a bowl; drain.

Bring 6 cups water to a boil in a saucepan and add the shrimp. Boil for 3 to 5 minutes or until shrimp turn pink. Rinse with cold water; drain. Peel and devein the shrimp.

Combine the cooked shrimp, orzo, artichoke hearts, bell pepper, basil and oregano in a large salad bowl. Toss with the Balsamic Vinaigrette.

To serve, arrange 1 cup of the salad greens on a plate. Top with some of the asparagus spears. Spoon the prepared shrimp and orzo mixture over the asparagus. Sprinkle with the Parmesan cheese.

Yield: 6 servings

CAN CAN CHICKEN

One of our testers was so impressed with the rich, golden color of this grilled chicken that she sent us pictures of it! She also shared that any soda can be substituted for the beer, if desired.

1 (3-pound) chicken
Soy sauce
Garlic powder

Seasonings of choice
1 can of beer

Rinse the chicken inside and out and pat dry; trim off excess fat. Rub the chicken with the soy sauce, garlic powder and other seasonings. Open the can of beer with a can opener to remove the entire top. Stand the chicken over the can of beer with the feet on either side of the can, resting on the grill. Close the lid and grill over hot coals on low for 1 hour to 1 hour and 15 minutes.

Yield: 4 servings

CHICKEN BOURSIN BUNDLES

Short on preparation time and long on flavor, these puff pastry bundles won our hearts. Prepare in advance and refrigerate or freeze to enjoy another time.

4 ounces Boursin garlic and
herb cheese blend
2 cups chopped cooked chicken
1 tablespoon chopped onion
2 tablespoons milk
Salt and pepper to taste

1 package frozen puff pastry,
thawed
1 egg, beaten
1 teaspoon water
3 tablespoons bread crumbs or
grated Parmesan cheese

Combine the Boursin cheese, chicken, onion, milk, salt and pepper in a bowl and mix well. Roll out the puff pastry into 1 large square. Cut into 4 squares. Spoon 1/4 of the chicken mixture into the center of each pastry square. Bring the 4 corners together in the center, pinching seams to seal. Beat the egg with the water in a small bowl. Brush the top of each pastry bundle with the egg wash. Sprinkle the bread crumbs over the top of each bundle. Arrange the bundles on a baking sheet. Bake at 350 degrees for 20 to 25 minutes or until golden brown.

Yield: 4 servings

SAVORY CHICKEN CREPES

These are absolutely luscious. They are light with full flavor, a good choice for showers or luncheons. The recipe makes more than enough crepes. Store the extras in the refrigerator or freeze them for later use. They are delicious heated up for breakfast filled with fresh fruit and whipped cream.

CREPES

2 cups flour	4 eggs
1/2 teaspoon salt	2 tablespoons vegetable oil
3 cups milk	

FILLING AND SAUCE

1 tablespoon minced shallots	2 egg yolks
8 1/2 tablespoons butter, divided	1/4 cup heavy cream
2 cups chopped cooked chicken	3/4 cup shredded Swiss cheese
1/2 cup white wine or sherry	1/2 cup grated Parmesan cheese
5 1/2 tablespoons flour, divided	Nutmeg, cayenne pepper, salt
1/2 cup hot chicken stock	and white pepper to taste
2 cups milk, divided	

For the crepes, combine the flour and salt in a large bowl. Whisk the milk, eggs and oil in a bowl. Add to the flour mixture, whisking slowly until smooth. Heat a small skillet or crepe pan sprayed with nonstick cooking spray over medium heat. Pour 2 to 3 tablespoons of crepe batter into the pan, tilting the pan to coat the bottom. Cook for 2 minutes; flip the crepe and cook for 30 seconds on the other side. Remove to waxed paper to cool. Repeat with remaining batter to make about 24 crepes.

For the filling, sauté the shallots in 2 tablespoons butter in a skillet until tender. Add the chicken and wine. Bring to a boil; reduce the heat. Simmer until the liquid has evaporated. Melt 2 tablespoons butter in a heavy saucepan. Whisk in 2 1/2 tablespoons flour until smooth. Add the chicken stock and 1/2 cup milk. Cook until thickened, whisking constantly; remove from the heat. Beat 1 egg yolk and the cream in a small mixing bowl; whisk gradually into the chicken stock mixture. Stir in 1/4 cup Swiss cheese and the prepared chicken mixture. Season with salt and pepper. Spoon about 1/4 cup chicken mixture into the center of each crepe. Roll up and place, seam side down, in a greased 9×13-inch baking dish.

For the sauce, melt 2 1/2 tablespoons butter in a saucepan. Whisk in 3 tablespoons flour until smooth. Add 1 1/2 cups milk. Cook until thickened, whisking constantly. Add 1 egg yolk and mix well. Add 1/2 cup Swiss cheese, the Parmesan cheese and 2 tablespoons butter; mix well. Stir in the nutmeg, cayenne pepper, salt and pepper. Pour the sauce over the crepes. Bake at 350 degrees for 20 to 25 minutes.

Yield: 10 to 12 servings

CHICKEN PROSCIUTTO LASAGNA

*This defines comfort food to us. The creamy rosemary Parmesan sauce with tender
chicken and smoky prosciutto feels like a blanket wrapped around you. If you want to save time,
buy a prepared roasted chicken at the grocery store.*

4 chicken breasts	1/2 teaspoon rosemary
1 1/4 cups chicken broth	1/2 teaspoon tarragon
1 cup water	1/2 teaspoon Beau Monde
3/4 cup (1 1/2 sticks) butter	seasoning
1/2 cup minus 1/2 tablespoon	1 1/2 cups freshly grated good-
flour	quality Parmesan cheese
2 cups milk	16 ounces lasagna noodles,
1 1/2 cups heavy cream	cooked
1/2 teaspoon salt	1/4 pound thinly sliced prosciutto
Nutmeg to taste	Chopped fresh parsley

Combine the chicken, chicken broth and water in a large stockpot. Bring to a boil and simmer
for 30 minutes or until the chicken juices run clear when pierced with a fork. Drain, reserving 1 cup
cooking liquid for the sauce. Cut the chicken into bite-size pieces; set aside.

Melt the butter in a saucepan. Whisk in the flour until smooth. Cook over medium heat for
3 minutes, stirring constantly. Add the milk, cream and reserved cooking liquid; reduce the heat to low.
Cook until thickened, stirring constantly. Stir in the salt, nutmeg, rosemary, tarragon, Beau Monde
seasoning and Parmesan cheese. Grease the bottom of a 9×13-inch lasagna pan. Spread a thin layer of
sauce over the bottom. Layer the noodles, sauce, chicken and prosciutto, ending with a layer of noodles
and sauce. Bake at 350 degrees for 25 to 30 minutes or until bubbly. Top with the parsley. Let stand for
a few minutes before serving.

Yield: 8 to 10 servings

WHITE BEAN CHICKEN CHILI

This was a hit at all our tastings. There is a wonderful layering of flavors and spices that we know you'll enjoy. Add a little crunch and garnish with thin strips of corn tortillas that have been fried until crisp and drained.

1 pound Great Northern beans
2 tablespoons vegetable oil
1 onion, chopped
2 carrots, chopped
2 ribs celery, chopped
3 garlic cloves, minced
2 (4-ounce) cans chopped green chiles
2 teaspoons ground cumin
1 1/2 teaspoons cayenne pepper
1 teaspoon oregano
1/2 teaspoon salt
2 pounds chicken breasts
1 (14-ounce) can reduced-sodium chicken broth

Sort and rinse the beans. Soak the beans overnight according to the package directions; drain. Place the beans in a stockpot and cover with 2 inches of water. Cook over low heat for 2 to 3 hours or until the beans are soft and the liquid is absorbed.

Heat the oil in a stockpot. Add the onion, carrots, celery and garlic. Sauté for 5 minutes or until the vegetables are tender. Add the chiles, cumin, cayenne pepper, oregano and salt; mix well. Add the chicken, chicken broth and enough water to cover. Bring to a boil and reduce the heat to low. Cook, covered, for 20 minutes or until the juices run clear when pierced with a fork. Remove the chicken and let cool to the touch. Cut the chicken into bite-size pieces, discarding the skin and bones.

Return the chicken to the pot. Cook over low heat for about 20 minutes. Add the beans and any bean liquid to the chicken mixture. Add additional water if necessary to achieve the desired consistency. Ladle into warmed bowls to serve. Serve accompaniments such as chopped scallions, shredded Cheddar cheese, sour cream and crispy tortilla strips in separate bowls. You may substitute 7 cups of rinsed, drained, canned beans for the dried beans.

Yield: 8 servings

CHICKEN CLUB SALAD WITH BASIL MAYONNAISE

One of our favorite sandwiches from childhood, updated into a glorious salad. If you miss the sandwich version too much, omit the croutons and pile it on a roll or bun. The leftover Basil Mayonnaise would be delicious on grilled burgers or spread on fresh fish, covered with bread crumbs, and baked.

CROUTONS

3 cups Italian bread cubes
3 tablespoons olive oil

Salt to taste

BASIL MAYONNAISE

1 cup mayonnaise
2 cups loosely packed basil leaves
1 garlic clove

4 teaspoons fresh lemon juice
1/2 teaspoon salt

SALAD

3 pounds chicken breasts,
cooked, cut into
bite-size pieces
1 pint cherry or grape tomatoes,
halved
4 scallions, finely chopped
(including green tops)

6 slices bacon, crisp-cooked,
crumbled
Salt to taste
Pepper to taste
Basil leaves

For the croutons, place the bread cubes in a bowl. Drizzle with the olive oil and toss to coat well; season with salt. Spread on a baking sheet. Toast at 350 degrees for 15 to 20 minutes or until golden brown; let cool.

For the mayonnaise, combine the mayonnaise, basil, garlic, lemon juice and salt in a blender. Process until well blended. Store in an airtight container in the refrigerator until serving time.

For the salad, combine the chicken, tomatoes, scallions and 2/3 of the bacon in a large salad bowl. Add 1/2 cup Basil Mayonnaise, salt and pepper; toss to mix well. Arrange the salad on 6 salad plates. Top each salad with some of the croutons, the remaining bacon and a few basil leaves. Serve immediately.

Yield: 6 servings

SOMBRERO CHICKEN SALAD

Inspired by the flavors of the Southwest, this is a do-ahead must. The Cilantro Lime Dressing doubles as the marinade for the chicken.

CILANTRO LIME DRESSING

1/2 cup lime juice	1 teaspoon ground cumin
1/3 cup vegetable oil	1/4 teaspoon salt
3/4 cup chopped fresh cilantro	1 garlic clove, minced

SALAD

1 boneless skinless chicken breast	1 (15-ounce) can black beans,
1 tomato, seeded, chopped	rinsed, drained
3 green onions, chopped	3/4 cup corn kernels
2 jalapeño chiles, seeded, minced	8 ounces pasta, cooked

Mix the lime juice, oil, cilantro, cumin, salt and garlic in a large bowl. Pour half of the dressing over the chicken in a glass bowl. Marinate the chicken, covered, in the refrigerator for at least 1 hour. Combine the tomato, green onions, jalapeño chiles, black beans, corn and cooked pasta with the remaining dressing in a bowl; mix well. Grill the chicken over hot coals for 10 minutes, basting with the marinade for the first 2 to 3 minutes; discard the marinade. Cut the chicken into bite-size pieces. Add to the salad, tossing to mix well. Serve chilled or at room temperature.

Yield: 5 servings

OPENING WINE

Buy a good corkscrew! Do not pick up the bottle and wave

it around while you carve away at the foil. Set the bottle

on a level surface and open it while it is flat on the surface.

An agitated wine doesn't taste so good.

ARROZ CON POLLO SALAD

A Spanish favorite, this version has been made into a salad destined for a special luncheon or dinner. Shrimp may be substituted for the chicken and peas for the green beans. The Tomato Garlic Mayonnaise is terrific with beef tenderloin or as a vegetable dip.

DRESSING

3 tablespoons fresh lemon juice
1 garlic clove, minced

1/4 teaspoon salt
1/2 cup extra-virgin olive oil

TOMATO GARLIC MAYONNAISE

2 garlic cloves, minced
1 cup mayonnaise

1 tablespoon tomato paste
2 teaspoons fresh lemon juice

SALAD

3 pounds cooked chicken,
cut into bite-size pieces
3 tablespoons vegetable oil
1 onion, finely chopped
2 cups uncooked long grain rice
1 (1-pound) ham steak,
cut into 1/2-inch cubes
1/2 teaspoon saffron

2 cups chicken broth
2 cups water
1/2 pound fresh green beans, cut
into 2-inch pieces
1 red bell pepper, julienned
3 scallions, sliced diagonally
(including green tops)

For the dressing, combine the lemon juice, garlic and salt in a bowl. Whisk in the olive oil until well blended. Store in a jar with a tight-fitting lid. Shake vigorously before serving.

For the mayonnaise, combine the garlic, mayonnaise, tomato paste and lemon juice in a bowl; mix well. Chill until serving time.

For the salad, combine the cooked chicken and 3 tablespoons of the dressing in a large bowl; set aside. Heat the oil in a large skillet. Sauté the onion in the hot oil until tender. Add the rice and sauté for 1 minute. Stir in the ham, saffron, chicken broth and water. Bring to a boil and reduce the heat to a simmer. Cook, covered, for 20 minutes or until the liquid is absorbed. Steam the green beans for 5 minutes; drain and rinse in cold water. Add the green beans and bell pepper to the hot rice; fluff the rice to mix. Remove from the heat and let stand, covered, for 5 minutes. Combine the rice mixture and remaining dressing in a large bowl. Toss to mix well and let cool. Stir in the prepared chicken. Spoon the salad into a large shallow bowl. Top with the sliced scallions. Serve with the Tomato Garlic Mayonnaise.

Yield: 8 to 10 servings

SMOKED TURKEY PASTA SALAD WITH DRIED CHERRY TOMATOES

This one-dish meal will be a welcome entrée at your next book club or Bunco Party.
All you need to add is fresh bread and a fruit salad.

VINAIGRETTE DRESSING

2 tablespoons chopped fresh cilantro	2 tablespoons white wine vinegar
1 tablespoon chopped fresh thyme	1 tablespoon balsamic vinegar
	1 tablespoon dry white wine
1 tablespoon chopped fresh basil	$1/2$ cup olive oil
2 shallots, minced	$1/4$ cup corn oil
1 garlic clove, minced	Salt and pepper to taste

SALAD

9 ounces fusilli pasta, cooked	1 small carrot, chopped
3 tablespoons olive oil	$1/2$ pound thick-sliced deli
$1/2$ cup cooked black beans	smoked turkey, cut into strips
$1/2$ red bell pepper, thinly sliced	1 cup oven-dried (or sun-dried)
$1/2$ yellow bell pepper, thinly sliced	cherry tomatoes, chopped
	1 garlic clove, minced
4 ounces fresh mozzarella cheese, cubed	1 tablespoon chopped fresh basil
	Salt and pepper to taste

For the dressing, combine the cilantro, thyme, basil, shallots and garlic in a small bowl. Whisk in the white wine vinegar, balsamic vinegar and wine. Add the olive oil and corn oil slowly, whisking until well blended. Season with salt and pepper; set aside.

For the salad, place the fusilli in a large serving bowl. Add the olive oil and toss to coat the pasta; let cool. Add the black beans, bell peppers, mozzarella cheese, carrot, turkey and dried tomatoes; mix well. Stir in the garlic and basil. Add the dressing and toss to coat well. Season with salt and pepper. Chill, covered, until serving time.

Note: To oven-dry tomatoes, combine 2 pints cherry or grape tomatoes with 2 to 3 tablespoons olive oil, tossing to coat well. Spread in a single layer on a baking sheet. Bake at 300 degrees (or lower) for 1 to 2 hours or until shriveled and light brown.

Yield: 6 to 8 servings

GRILLED DUCK WITH RASPBERRY CARDAMOM VANILLA BEAN SAUCE

Another showstopper from Chef Marty Blitz of the Mise en Place Restaurant. Here he pairs duck with a sweet raspberry sauce that is infused with scents of India. This can also be prepared with chicken breasts.

SAUCE
1 pint fresh or frozen raspberries
1/2 cup sugar
6 cardamom pods, crushed
1 vanilla bean, inside scraped
2 tablespoons rice vinegar
1 teaspoon orange zest
1 cup water

DUCK
4 (6-ounce) duck breasts
Salt to taste
Pepper to taste
1/4 teaspoon garam masala

For the sauce, combine the raspberries, sugar, cardamom pods, vanilla bean, rice vinegar, orange zest and water in a saucepan. Bring to a boil. Reduce the heat and simmer for 15 minutes; strain. Return the sauce to the saucepan and reduce until slightly thickened.

For the duck, season the duck breasts with salt, pepper and garam masala. Grill the duck over hot coals, skin side down, until crispy. Grill on the other side for 1 minute. Remove to a baking dish. Bake at 450 degrees for 3 minutes. Let stand for 5 minutes before slicing.

Serve the duck with the sauce and garnish with chopped fresh cilantro.

Note: Garam masala is a blend of spices used in Indian cooking. It can be found at specialty cooking shops and some grocery stores.

Yield: 4 servings

PARTY STEAK SPIRAL

Roasted sweet red peppers, basil, and prosciutto combine with the steak to create a marvelous dish for entertaining. Slice and fan out on individual plates or a large platter for a buffet.

MARINADE

1/2 cup olive oil	1 tablespoon chopped fresh
1/4 cup red wine vinegar	parsley
2 garlic cloves, minced	1/4 teaspoon ground pepper

STEAK

1 (1 1/4-pound) flank steak, butterflied	24 basil leaves
2 roasted red bell peppers, cut into 4 halves	3 tablespoons grated Parmesan cheese
1 tablespoon chopped fresh parsley	2 tablespoons chopped fresh parsley
6 to 8 thin slices prosciutto	Freshly ground pepper to taste

For the marinade, combine the olive oil, red wine vinegar, garlic, parsley and pepper in a shallow glass dish.

For the steak, add the steak to the marinade. Marinate, covered, in the refrigerator for 2 to 8 hours.

Remove the steak from the marinade to a foil-covered work surface, reserving marinade. Place the bell pepper halves on top of the steak. Sprinkle with 1 tablespoon parsley and cover with the prosciutto slices. Arrange the basil leaves in a single layer over the prosciutto. Sprinkle with the Parmesan cheese, 2 tablespoons parsley and pepper.

Lifting the steak away from the foil, roll tightly from the long side as for a jelly roll. Tie the steak tightly with kitchen string at 2- to 3-inch intervals. Place the steak in a shallow baking dish and pour the reserved marinade over the steak. Bake at 400 degrees for 30 to 45 minutes (for medium-rare to medium) or to the desired doneness, basting twice during cooking. Let stand for 15 minutes before slicing.

To serve, cut into 1/2-inch slices, removing the string as you cut. Arrange on a platter.

Yield: 6 to 8 servings

CLASSIC BEEF TENDERLOIN

Beef tenderloin seems to be the perfect choice for entertaining: You can make it ahead, it is great served hot or cold, and it is versatile as a main course or sliced very thin atop crostini.

1 (4- to 5-pound) beef tenderloin   Salt and pepper to taste
1 garlic clove, cut into slivers

Fold the ends of the tenderloin under and tie with kitchen string so that the entire roast is a uniform thickness. Cut a few slits in the tenderloin and insert the garlic slivers. Season generously with salt and pepper. Arrange the tenderloin in a roasting pan. Roast at 425 degrees for 10 minutes. Reduce the temperature to 350 degrees. Roast for 25 minutes (rare) or 35 minutes (medium). Let stand for 15 minutes before slicing.

Yield: 8 servings

DEAD SERIOUS CHILI

This contributor's husband has been cooking competition chili for 10 years nationwide. He cooks out of a rebuilt coffin with a burner, cutting board, and cooler, hence the name Dead Serious Chili.

4 pounds sirloin steak,   2 cups chili powder
cut into 1/4-inch cubes   3 green chiles, chopped
1 pound bulk pork sausage   4 tablespoons ground cumin
1 onion, chopped   1 teaspoon cilantro
3 garlic cloves, minced   1/2 teaspoon oregano
Salt to taste   2 scotch bonnet chiles, or
1 (16-ounce) can tomato sauce   1 teaspoon cayenne pepper
4 (14-ounce) cans beef stock   (optional)

Brown the beef and sausage in an iron skillet with the onion, garlic and salt, stirring until the sausage is crumbly and the onion is tender; drain. Spoon into a large stockpot. Add the tomato sauce and 2 cans of beef stock. Bring to a boil, reduce the heat and simmer for 1 hour. Add the chili powder, green chiles, cumin, cilantro, oregano and remaining beef stock. Float the scotch bonnet chiles on the top; do not cut into the chiles. Cook over low heat for 45 minutes. Remove the chiles before serving.

Yield: 15 to 20 generous servings

FIESTA PIE WITH CHIPOTLE CORN BREAD TOPPING

An all-in-one dish, great when entertaining family or doubled for a crowd.
Try the chipotle topping for a hot, smoky flavor.

CHIPOTLE CORN BREAD TOPPING
1/3 cup milk
1 egg
1/2 cup sour cream
1/4 cup (1/2 stick) butter, melted
3 chipotle chiles, seeded, chopped
1 package corn muffin mix

FIESTA PIE
1 pound ground beef
1/3 cup chopped green bell pepper
1/3 cup chopped onion
1 garlic clove, minced
1 cup mild chunky salsa
1 cup frozen white corn kernels
1 envelope taco seasoning mix
1/2 cup shredded Cheddar cheese

For the corn bread topping, mix the milk, egg, sour cream, melted butter and chiles in a bowl. Add the corn muffin mix and stir just until combined.

For the pie, brown the ground beef in a skillet, stirring until crumbly; drain. Add the bell pepper, onion and garlic. Cook until tender. Stir in the salsa, corn and seasoning mix. Spoon into a round baking dish. Spoon the corn bread batter over the top. Bake at 375 degrees for 30 to 40 minutes or until a wooden pick inserted in the corn bread comes out clean. Sprinkle the Cheddar cheese over the top of the corn bread. Bake until the cheese is melted and bubbly. You may substitute ground turkey for the ground beef if desired.

The corn bread topping can also be made into muffins. Fill muffin tins half full and bake at 375 degrees for 15 minutes.

Yield: 4 servings

ASIAN PORK TENDERLOIN

The rich flavors in this pork tenderloin belie the ease with which it is put together. Sliced thinly and topped with the sweet mustard, this also makes a great sandwich or topping for crostini.

PORK

1/2 cup soy sauce	1 teaspoon sesame oil
1/4 cup honey	1/2 teaspoon Chinese five-spice
3 garlic cloves, minced	powder
2 tablespoons rice wine vinegar	Juice of 1 orange
1 tablespoon dry sherry	1 (3- to 4-pound) pork
2 teaspoons minced fresh	tenderloin
gingerroot	

SWEET MUSTARD SAUCE

1/2 cup Dijon mustard	1 teaspoon minced fresh
2 tablespoons peanut oil	gingerroot
1 1/2 tablespoons sugar	Salt and pepper to taste
1 teaspoon sesame oil	

For the pork, combine the soy sauce, honey, garlic, rice wine vinegar, sherry, gingerroot, sesame oil, five-spice powder and orange juice in a shallow glass dish. Add the tenderloin. Marinate, in the refrigerator, for 2 to 3 hours. Remove the tenderloin, discarding the marinade. Grill over hot coals until the pork tests done on a meat thermometer. You may also roast at 400 degrees for 10 minutes per pound. Let stand for a few minutes before slicing. Serve with the Sweet Mustard Sauce. You may also serve the tenderloin slices on rolls with Asian Slaw (page 57) for mini sandwiches.

For the sauce, whisk the Dijon mustard, peanut oil, sugar, sesame oil and gingerroot in a small bowl. Season with salt and pepper. Chill, covered, until serving time.

Yield: 6 servings

PULLED PARTY PORK

You can be out running errands, shopping, or at work while the slow cooker does the cooking for you. Serve on soft rolls with coleslaw and chips for your next game day party.

1 (3-pound) pork tenderloin or Boston butt roast
1 cup water
1 (18-ounce) bottle prepared barbecue sauce

1/4 cup packed brown sugar
2 tablespoons Worcestershire sauce
1 teaspoon each salt and pepper

Combine the pork and water in a slow cooker. Cook on High for 7 hours. Drain, reserving 1 cup liquid. Shred the roast in the slow cooker with a fork. Add the remaining ingredients. Add the reserved cooking liquid if necessary. Cook on Low for 1 hour. Serve on rolls for sandwiches if desired.

Yield: 8 to 10 servings

DINNER PARTY RACK OF LAMB

Pecans, honey mustard, and bread crumbs create a crispy topping for these succulent lamb chops. Have your butcher French the bones for you for the best result.

1 rack of lamb per couple
1/2 teaspoon kosher salt
Pepper to taste
Olive oil for drizzling
1/4 cup honey mustard
2 cups coarse bread crumbs

1 cup chopped pecans
2 tablespoons extra-virgin olive oil
1 tablespoon chopped fresh parsley
1/2 teaspoon thyme or marjoram

Trim the fat from the lamb and French strip the bones. Season with salt and pepper on both sides. Place bone side up in a roasting pan. Drizzle with olive oil. Roast at 425 degrees for 15 minutes. Spread the honey mustard on the lamb. Combine the bread crumbs, pecans, 2 tablespoons olive oil, parsley and thyme in a small bowl. Press the bread crumb mixture into the mustard layer. Broil the lamb until the bread crumbs are brown. Let cool before slicing between the bones to serve.

Yield: 1 rack per couple

BLACK BEAN VEGETABLE WRAPS

Use red or green flour tortillas to wrap around this colorful filling of vegetables and black beans. Wrapped in parchment, these will travel well for lunch on the beach or a tailgate party.

16 ounces cream cheese,
   softened
2 cups shredded Pepper
   Jack cheese
1/2 cup sour cream
1 teaspoon onion salt
2 (15-ounce) cans black beans,
   rinsed, drained
1/4 cup salsa

12 (8-inch) flour tortillas
   (regular, spinach or red
   pepper)
10 ounces fresh spinach
2 (7-ounce) jars roasted sweet
   red peppers, drained,
   chopped
2 carrots, shredded (optional)

Combine the cream cheese, Pepper Jack cheese, sour cream and onion salt in a mixing bowl; beat until well blended. Process the black beans and salsa in a food processor until smooth. Spread the bean mixture in a light layer over each tortilla. Top evenly with the cheese mixture, spinach, red peppers and carrots. Roll up the tortillas tightly. Wrap in plastic wrap and chill before serving. Serve with a side of salsa and sour cream for dipping. You may add sliced grilled chicken or steak if desired.

Yield: 12 wraps

WINE AND SPICY ETHNIC DISHES

For Asian, Mexican, or Middle Eastern plates, dry to off-dry whites are the best marriage partners. Look for Gewürztraminer or Pinot Gris from Alsace, New Zealand Riesling or Sauvignon Blanc, or for something different, Chateauneuf-du-Pape Blanc from the Rhone Valley.

BLACK BEAN TART WITH CHILI CRUST

Black beans are a well-loved part of Tampa's Spanish and Cuban culture. This recipe elevates them in a savory tart that can hold its own as an entrée or a side dish.

CRUST

1 1/4 cups flour
1 teaspoon ground cumin
1 teaspoon chili powder
1 teaspoon paprika

1/2 teaspoon salt
1/2 cup (1 stick) cold butter,
    cut into pats
2 tablespoons ice water

FILLING

3 cups canned black beans,
    rinsed, drained
2 tablespoons sour cream
1 tablespoon vegetable oil
1 red onion, chopped
1 (10-ounce) package frozen
    corn, thawed

1 cup chopped red bell pepper
1/2 cup chopped scallions
1/2 cup chopped fresh cilantro
2 jalapeño chiles, seeded, finely
    chopped
1 1/2 cups shredded Monterey
    Jack cheese

For the crust, combine the flour, cumin, chili powder, paprika and salt in a food processor. Add the butter and pulse until the consistency of coarse meal. Add the ice water and process until a dough forms. Press the dough evenly on the bottom and side of a 10-inch tart pan. Chill for 15 minutes. Line the pan with foil and fill with pie weights or dried beans. Bake at 350 degrees for 8 to 10 minutes or until the edge begins to brown. Remove the foil and pie weights. Bake for 10 minutes or until golden brown; let cool.

For the filling, combine 1 cup of the black beans and the sour cream in a food processor. Purée until smooth. Heat the oil in a skillet. Sauté the onion and corn until tender. Combine the corn mixture in a large bowl with the remaining 2 cups black beans, bell pepper, scallions, cilantro, jalapeño chiles and Monterey Jack cheese; mix well. Spread the puréed beans over the prepared tart shell. Spoon the corn mixture over the prepared layer. Bake at 350 degrees until bubbly and the cheese is melted. Serve with lime sour cream.

Note: To make lime sour cream, combine 1 cup sour cream and 2 teaspoons fresh lime juice in a bowl and mix well. Chill until serving time.

Yield: 6 to 8 servings

BRIE AND SAUSAGE BRUNCH SOUFFLÉ

*Mild Brie, spicy sausage, and fresh sage team up to create a meal you will
remember long after leaving the table.*

6 slices white bread	2 cups milk
1 pound hot bulk pork sausage, browned, drained	1 1/2 tablespoons chopped fresh sage
3/4 pound Brie cheese, rind removed, cubed	1 teaspoon seasoned salt
	1 teaspoon dry mustard
1 cup grated Parmesan cheese	2 eggs
5 eggs	1 cup whipping cream
2 cups whipping cream	

Trim the crusts from the bread slices and place the crusts evenly on the bottom of a lightly
greased 9×13-inch baking dish. Layer the bread slices, sausage, Brie and Parmesan cheese in the baking
dish. Whisk 5 eggs and 2 cups whipping cream in a bowl. Add the milk, sage, seasoned salt and dry
mustard and mix well. Pour over the bread layers. Chill, covered, for 8 hours. Whisk 2 eggs and 1 cup
whipping cream in a bowl. Pour over the prepared layers. Bake at 350 degrees for 1 hour or until the
center is set and a knife inserted in the center comes out clean. You may substitute half-and-half for the
whipping cream if desired.

Yield: 8 to 10 servings

STORING WINE

Some wines are for drinking young; others are for aging. Unless you

have access to a cool space (55 degrees, 75% humidity) buy only

enough wine to enjoy over a few months. If you are unsure of

whether a wine is ready to drink, err on the side of youth.

GOOD MORNING PASTRY POCKET

*We love food that looks like we spent all day on it, but actually took only a few minutes
to prepare. Try the pastry with fruit filling dusted with confectioners' sugar for dessert or fill it
with leftover chicken, vegetables, and cheese for a quick dinner.*

1/2 roll of hot bulk pork sausage
1/2 medium onion, finely chopped
2 tablespoons butter
6 eggs, beaten
1 sheet frozen puff pastry, thawed
3/4 cup shredded Cheddar cheese

Brown the sausage in a skillet, stirring until crumbly; drain. Spoon the cooked sausage into a large
bowl. Add the onion to the skillet and sauté until tender. Spoon the onion into the bowl with the
sausage. Melt the butter in the skillet and add the eggs. Scramble the eggs until cooked through and
spoon into the bowl. Mix well and let cool. The egg mixture may be prepared 1 day in advance and
stored, covered, in the refrigerator until ready to prepare the pastry.

Roll the thawed pastry out onto a parchment-lined baking sheet. Add the Cheddar cheese to the
egg mixture and mix well. Spoon the filling lengthwise down the center of the pastry. Fold in the sides
to cover the filling and seal the ends with a middle seam. Bake at 400 degrees for 30 minutes or until
puffed and golden brown. Cut into slices to serve.

Yield: 4 to 6 servings

THE LIFE OF THE PARTY

GRAND FINALES

CULINARY COLLECTION

STRAWBERRY AND CREAM SANDWICHES

For a spectacular finish to your luncheon or dinner party, try this submission from one of Tampa's finest chefs, Rob Stanford of the Tampa Yacht & Country Club. This is a cookie that you build complete desserts around. The cookies are wonderful on their own, but you can also try shaping the cookie while still warm into a cup using a muffin cup or an upside-down ramekin.

NUT LACE COOKIES

3/4 cup blanched almonds   3/4 cup sugar
2 tablespoons flour   2 1/2 ounces (2/3 stick) butter,
1 tablespoon milk   softened, cut into pieces

RASPBERRY SAUCE AND ASSEMBLY

1 pound frozen raspberries, thawed   Sliced strawberries
1 cup raspberry preserves   Fresh mint leaves
1 cup whipping cream   Confectioners' sugar
2 tablespoons sugar

For the cookies, process the almonds and flour in a food processor until very finely ground. Add the milk, sugar and butter. Process for 8 seconds or until the mixture forms a ball. Line a cookie sheet with parchment paper that has been lightly greased on both sides. Using 2 teaspoons of batter for each cookie, shape into balls and press down onto the parchment paper. To ensure perfectly round cookies, pay special attention to the roundness of the shaped balls. Bake at 350 degrees for 12 minutes. The dough should spread evenly and cookies should be brown. They will become crisp as they cool.

For the sauce, press the raspberries and preserves through a fine mesh strainer into a bowl to remove the seeds. Mix well.

For the assembly, beat the whipping cream and sugar in a small mixing bowl until stiff peaks form. Spoon the whipped cream into a pastry bag fitted with a decorator tip. Spoon about 1 tablespoon of the raspberry sauce onto 8 dessert plates. Pipe a small dot of the whipped cream in the center of the sauce and press 1 cookie into it, ensuring that the cookie sits above the sauce without sliding. Pipe 5 dots of whipped cream around the outside edge of the cookie and a small amount in the center of the cookie. Arrange strawberries decoratively around the edge of the cookie, in between the whipped cream dots and in the center of the cookie. Top with another cookie, pipe whipped cream in the center and decorate with strawberries and fresh mint. Sprinkle with confectioners' sugar and serve immediately. The cookies can be made in advance and stored in an airtight container. Assemble the dessert immediately before serving.

Yield: 8 servings

PEACHES AND BERRIES WITH CREAMY GRAND MARNIER SAUCE

Present this in a trifle bowl with layers of berries and cream or in individual compotes for your next elegant summer meal.

SAUCE
10 ounces cream cheese, softened
1 cup sour cream
1/2 cup plus 6 tablespoons confectioners' sugar
1/2 cup whipping cream
1 teaspoon orange zest
1/8 teaspoon vanilla extract
2 tablespoons (or more) Grand Marnier

ASSEMBLY
6 to 8 cups sliced mixed fresh fruit,
such as peaches, strawberries, raspberries and blueberries
Fresh mint leaves

For the sauce, combine the cream cheese, sour cream, confectioners' sugar, whipping cream, orange zest and vanilla in a blender. Process until smooth. Add the Grand Marnier and process until well blended. You may add more Grand Marnier to taste. Chill for 1 hour before serving.

For the assembly, spoon the fresh fruit into 8 Champagne glasses, martini glasses or any stemmed dessert dishes. Spoon the sauce over the fruit and top with a mint leaf. Serve immediately.

Yield: 8 servings

BANANAS FOSTER

We just couldn't resist this New Orleans classic. To make ahead, scoop the ice cream into four dessert bowls and freeze. You may prepare the sauce up until the bananas are added and chill. Just before serving, warm the sauce, add the bananas, and serve over the ice cream.

1/2 cup (1 stick) butter	Dash of 151 rum
1 cup packed brown sugar	Dash of cinnamon
1/4 cup banana liqueur	4 firm bananas, sliced
1/4 cup dark rum	Vanilla ice cream

Melt the butter in a skillet. Stir in the brown sugar. Cook until melted and well blended. Add the banana liqueur, dark rum, 151 rum, cinnamon and bananas. Cook until the bananas are warm and softened; do not let bananas get mushy.

Scoop the ice cream into dessert bowls and top with the hot banana mixture. Serve immediately.

You may also use the recipe for Nut Lace Cookies (page 100) and follow the directions for making the cookie cup. Serve the ice cream in the cookie cup and top with the warm banana sauce.

Yield: 4 servings

WINES TO SERVE WITH DESSERT

Try to look for wines that have an affinity for the dessert you are

serving. Lively, lighter grape varieties like Vouvray from the Loire or

Riesling from Germany work great with salty cheese and fresh fruit.

Rich, thick wines like Port cry out for chocolate.

PEARS IN MASCARPONE CUSTARD

This was inspired by a Tuscan favorite. Peaches or apples could be substituted depending on the season. Try preparing this in individual ramekins for an elegant dinner club finale.

6 medium pears
Juice of 1 lemon
1/4 cup sugar
1/4 cup (1/2 stick) butter, softened
1/2 cup sugar
1 egg
2/3 cup mascarpone cheese
2 tablespoons flour

Peel and slice the pears; place in a bowl. Sprinkle with the lemon juice. Arrange in a greased baking dish. Sprinkle with 1/4 cup sugar. Beat the butter and 1/2 cup sugar in a mixing bowl until light and fluffy. Beat in the egg and mascarpone cheese. Stir in the flour. Spoon over the pear slices. Bake at 350 degrees for 20 minutes or until the custard is set.

Yield: 6 servings

AFTER-DINNER DRINKS

After a wonderful dinner, many hosts find themselves wondering

what to serve their guests to drink. There are the standbys

of port, cognac, or dessert wines, which are always well received.

Throughout the chapter we have included other ideas to help

perpetuate the festivities and stand in for a dessert if needed.

CAPPUCCINO FLAN

Flan is a popular Spanish dessert in the Tampa area. This one is flavored with coffee and bathed in a rich caramel sauce. Serve this on a footed cake plate after enjoying a dinner of Spanish specialties, such as Roasted Pork or Chicken and Yellow Rice. Garnish with chocolate-covered coffee beans.

1 cup sugar
1 (14-ounce) can evaporated milk
1 (14-ounce) can sweetened condensed milk
1 cup whole milk
5 eggs
1 egg yolk
1 teaspoon vanilla extract
1 teaspoon instant coffee granules dissolved in
1 teaspoon boiling water
2 tablespoons coffee-flavored liqueur, such as Kahlúa

Heat the sugar in a heavy saucepan over medium heat. As the sugar begins to melt, pick up the pan and swirl to coat the bottom or stir with a wooden spoon. Heat until golden and caramelized. Pour into a warm pie plate; set aside. Place the saucepan in hot water immediately to prevent the caramelized sugar from sticking to the pan.

Combine the evaporated milk, sweetened condensed milk, whole milk, eggs, egg yolk, vanilla, coffee mixture and coffee liqueur in a blender. Process on low for 1 minute. Pour over the caramelized sugar in the pie plate. Place the pie plate in a large roasting pan and place on the middle rack in the oven. Pour boiling water into the pan 1 inch deep. Bake at 325 degrees in the water bath for 30 to 35 minutes or until the custard is set. Remove pie plate to a wire rack to cool. Chill at least 6 hours before serving.

To serve, run a thin knife around the edge of the pan to loosen the custard. Invert onto a serving plate, letting caramel run over the top of the custard. Cut into wedges to serve.

Yield: 8 servings

CHOCOLATE BREAD PUDDING

This comes from an old English family recipe brought to Long Island, New York, in the early 1800s. Our member's family made this only for very special occasions.

3 cups whole milk
3 ounces unsweetened chocolate, or 9 tablespoons baking cocoa and
3 tablespoons shortening
4 slices dry white bread, crusts trimmed, cubed
3 eggs
1 cup sugar
1 teaspoon vanilla extract
1/4 teaspoon salt

Scald the milk and chocolate in a saucepan, stirring constantly. Pour over the bread cubes in a greased 1-quart baking dish. Set aside to cool. Beat the eggs, sugar, vanilla and salt in a mixing bowl until well blended. Pour over the bread mixture. Place the dish in a large roasting pan. Add water to fill half way up the side of the dish. Bake at 350 degrees for 1 hour and 10 minutes or until a knife inserted in the center comes out clean. Serve warm with hard sauce of choice.

To make traditional hard sauce, combine 1 cup confectioners' sugar, 5 tablespoons butter, 1 tablespoon rum, 1 teaspoon vanilla extract and 1/8 teaspoon salt in a mixing bowl. Beat until smooth and creamy.

Yield: 6 to 8 servings

ESPRESSO MARTINI

Combine 2 ounces Irish cream, 2 ounces Kahlúa, a splash of Grand Marnier, 2 ounces espresso or strong coffee and 1 ounce premium vodka in a cocktail shaker. Add crushed ice, cover and shake vigorously. Strain and serve straight up in martini glasses. Yield: 2 servings.

Molten Chocolate Lava Cakes

A very committed member experimented extensively to find just the right recipe for this popular restaurant dessert. We applaud her efforts and hope you'll enjoy these warm cakes with molten centers as much as we do. The beauty in these is that they can easily be made ahead, chilled, and baked just prior to serving.

THYME WHIPPED CREAM
1 cup whipping cream
2 teaspoons dried thyme

CAKES
Butter
Flour
5 ounces bittersweet chocolate, chopped
3/4 cup (1 1/2 sticks) butter, cut into pats
4 egg yolks
1/4 cup sugar
3 tablespoons flour
4 egg whites
1/4 cup sugar

For the whipped cream, beat the whipping cream and thyme in a mixing bowl until stiff peaks form. Freeze until serving time.

For the cakes, butter 8 ramekins and freeze for 5 minutes; butter again. Dust with flour, shaking off the excess. Combine the chocolate and 3/4 cup butter in a double boiler over simmering water. Cook until melted and smooth, stirring constantly. Remove from the heat to cool. Beat the egg yolks and 1/4 cup sugar in a mixing bowl until pale yellow and thickened. Stir in the cooled chocolate mixture and 3 tablespoons flour. Beat the egg whites and 1/4 cup sugar in a mixing bowl until soft peaks form. Fold the meringue into the chocolate mixture. Spoon the mixture evenly into the ramekins. Chill, covered with plastic wrap, for 8 to 24 hours. Place the ramekins on a baking sheet. Bake at 400 degrees for 8 to 9 minutes or until puffed but not set in the center. Remove to a wire rack to cool for 10 minutes or until cakes fall slightly.

To serve, run a knife around the edge of the ramekins to loosen cakes. Invert onto dessert plates. Scoop out the frozen whipped cream with a small ice cream scoop and place on top of each cake. Serve immediately with a scoop of vanilla ice cream on the side.

Yield: 8 servings

CHOCOLATE CLOUD

After baking, this cake forms a crater that is the perfect spot to mound freshly whipped cream.
Dust with baking cocoa and sprinkle with raspberries to serve.

CAKE
8 ounces good-quality bittersweet or semisweet chocolate, coarsely chopped
1/2 cup (1 stick) unsalted butter, cut into pats and softened
1 egg
5 egg yolks
1/2 cup sugar
2 tablespoons liqueur (Frangelico, Grand Marnier or Kahlúa)
5 egg whites
1/2 cup sugar

WHIPPED CREAM
11/2 cups whipping cream, chilled
3 tablespoons confectioners' sugar
1 teaspoon vanilla extract

For the cake, line the bottom of an 8-inch springform pan with a round piece of waxed paper. Melt the chocolate in a microwave-safe bowl in the microwave. Stir in the butter until melted and well blended. You may also melt the chocolate and butter in a double boiler. Set aside.

Whisk the egg in a bowl with the egg yolks. Whisk in 1/2 cup sugar until pale yellow and thickened. Whisk in the melted chocolate mixture until well blended. Stir in the liqueur; set aside.

Beat the egg whites in a mixing bowl until foamy. Add 1/2 cup sugar gradually, beating until soft peaks form. Spoon about 1/4 of the meringue into the chocolate mixture. Fold in the remaining meringue. Pour the batter into the springform pan, smoothing the top.

Bake at 350 degrees for 40 minutes or until the top is puffed and begins to crack; do not overbake. Remove to a wire rack to cool; the top of the cake will fall slightly.

For the whipped topping, immediately before serving, beat the cream, confectioners' sugar and vanilla in a mixing bowl until stiff peaks form.

To serve, spoon the topping into the center of the cake. Run a knife around the side of the pan to loosen the cake. Remove the side from the pan and cut into slices to serve.

Yield: 8 to 12 servings

BLACK RUSSIAN CAKE

This is a decadent chocolate indulgence that combines a rich dessert with a popular after-dinner drink, the Black Russian. Try serving this with whipped cream or vanilla or coffee ice cream.

GLAZE
1/4 cup Kahlúa or coffee liqueur
1/4 cup vodka
1 1/2 cups confectioners' sugar

CAKE
1 (2-layer) package chocolate cake mix
1/2 cup sugar
1 cup sour cream
2/3 cup vegetable oil
4 eggs
1 tablespoon plus 1 teaspoon espresso granules
1 teaspoon vanilla extract
1 cup (6 ounces) milk chocolate chips
1 cup (6 ounces) mini chocolate chips

For the glaze, combine the Kahlúa, vodka and confectioners' sugar in a small bowl and whisk until smooth.

For the cake, combine the cake mix, sugar, sour cream and oil in a mixing bowl; beat until well blended. Add the eggs and beat for 3 to 4 minutes. Add the espresso granules and vanilla and mix well. Fold in the milk chocolate chips and the mini chocolate chips. Pour into a greased and floured bundt pan.

Bake at 350 degrees for 1 hour and 15 minutes or until the cake begins to pull away from the side of the pan and a wooden pick inserted in the center comes out clean. Cool on a wire rack for 10 minutes. Invert onto a serving plate. Pour the glaze over the warm cake.

This cake can be made 1 day in advance and chilled or frozen for several months.

Yield: 16 servings

CHOCOLATE CHIP CAKE

*The grated chocolate is the key to this light, moist cake. You might find yourself
making excuses to bake it.*

4 eggs
1 cup water
1/2 cup vegetable oil
1 (2-layer) package yellow cake mix
1 (4-ounce) package vanilla instant pudding mix
4 ounces semisweet chocolate, grated
1 cup (6 ounces) chocolate chips
Confectioners' sugar

Beat the eggs, water and oil in a mixing bowl. Add the cake mix and pudding mix gradually,
beating for 2 minutes. Stir in the grated chocolate and chocolate chips. Pour into a greased bundt pan.
Bake at 350 degrees for 45 to 55 minutes. Cool on a wire rack. Invert onto a serving plate.
Sprinkle with confectioners' sugar.

Yield: 16 servings

CHOCOLATINI

Combine 2 ounces Godiva chocolate liqueur, 2 ounces premium

vodka and a splash of raspberry liqueur in a cocktail shaker.

Add crushed ice, cover and shake vigorously. Strain into

chilled martini glasses. Yield: 2 servings.

CARAMEL APPLE CAKE

A great morning cake for a fall meeting or get-together. The tart apples and caramel icing are a classic combination.

CAKE
3 cups flour
2 teaspoons baking soda
1 teaspoon salt
1 teaspoon cinnamon
1 teaspoon nutmeg
1 cup packed brown sugar
1 cup sugar
3/4 cup vegetable oil
2 eggs
1 teaspoon vanilla extract
4 cups chopped Granny Smith apples (3 to 4 large apples)

GLAZE
1/2 cup (1 stick) butter
1 cup packed brown sugar
1/4 cup milk

For the cake, combine the flour, baking soda, salt, cinnamon and nutmeg in a bowl; set aside. Beat the brown sugar, sugar, oil, eggs and vanilla in a mixing bowl. Add the flour mixture to the sugar mixture and beat until well blended; mixture will be very thick. Fold in the apples. Pour into a greased and floured bundt pan. Bake at 350 degrees for 1 hour or until a wooden pick inserted in the center comes out clean. Cool on a wire rack. Invert onto a serving plate.

For the glaze, combine the butter, brown sugar and milk in a saucepan. Bring to a boil, reduce the heat and simmer for 2 minutes and 30 seconds. Pour the hot glaze over the cooled cake.

Yield: 12 servings

BERRY CRUMB CAKE

*A little crunch, sweet berries, and buttery cake make a delicious treat we would
love to serve for brunch, lunch, or a picnic.*

TOPPING
1^1/$_2$ cups flour
^{1}/$_2$ cup packed brown sugar
^{1}/$_4$ cup sugar
^{1}/$_2$ teaspoon salt
^{3}/$_4$ cup (1^1/$_2$ sticks) cold butter

CAKE
2^1/$_2$ cups flour
1 teaspoon baking soda
1 teaspoon baking powder
^{1}/$_4$ teaspoon salt
10 tablespoons butter, softened
1 cup sugar
3 eggs
1 teaspoon vanilla extract
1^1/$_4$ cups sour cream
1 cup blueberries
1 cup sliced strawberries
1 cup raspberries

For the topping, combine the flour, brown sugar, sugar and salt in a bowl or food processor. Cut in the butter or process until crumbly.

For the cake, combine the flour, baking soda, baking powder and salt in a bowl; set aside.

Beat the butter and sugar in a mixing bowl until light and fluffy. Add the eggs 1 at a time, beating well after each addition. Stir in the vanilla and sour cream. Add the flour mixture and mix just until combined. Spoon into a greased and floured 9-inch springform pan. Top with the blueberries, strawberries and raspberries, pressing gently into the batter. Sprinkle the crumb topping over the fruit. Bake at 350 degrees for 1 hour and 15 minutes. Cool on a wire rack. Remove the side from the pan and cut into slices to serve.

Yield: 12 servings

MACADAMIA CHEESECAKE

A cheesecake that melts in your mouth! The buttery graham cracker crust, rich nuts, and white chocolate can make this addictive. Garnish with additional macadamia nuts, drizzled white chocolate, or fresh berries.

CRUST
1 cup graham cracker crumbs
1/2 cup macadamia nuts, chopped
3 tablespoons sugar
1/3 cup melted butter

FILLING
16 ounces cream cheese, softened
1/2 cup sugar
1/2 teaspoon vanilla extract
2 eggs
1/2 cup chopped white chocolate
1/2 cup chopped macadamia nuts
1/2 cup chopped white chocolate

For the crust, mix the graham cracker crumbs, macadamia nuts, sugar and melted butter in a bowl. Press into the bottom and up the side of a 9-inch springform pan.

For the filling, beat the cream cheese, sugar and vanilla in a mixing bowl at medium speed until creamy and well blended. Add the eggs and beat well. Stir in 1/2 cup white chocolate. Pour into the prepared crust. Sprinkle the macadamia nuts and 1/2 cup white chocolate over the top. Bake at 350 degrees for 40 minutes. Cool on a wire rack. Chill for at least 3 hours before removing from the pan. Remove the side of the pan and cut into slices to serve.

Yield: 12 servings

CALYPSO PIE

The flavors of an iced coffee drink in a luscious ice cream pie.

CRUST
1 1/2 cups graham cracker crumbs
1/4 cup (1/2 stick) butter, melted

SAUCE
1/2 cup sugar
2 tablespoons baking cocoa
2/3 cup evaporated milk
1 tablespoon butter
1/2 teaspoon vanilla extract

FILLING AND ASSEMBLY
1/2 gallon coffee ice cream, softened
1/4 cup Kahlúa
3/4 cup slivered almonds, toasted
Whipped topping

For the crust, mix the graham cracker crumbs and melted butter in a bowl. Press into a greased pie plate; chill.

For the sauce, combine the sugar, baking cocoa and evaporated milk in a saucepan. Cook over medium heat until the mixture begins to boil, stirring constantly. Reduce the heat to low and simmer for 5 minutes. Remove from the heat and stir in the butter and vanilla. Pour into a bowl and chill.

For the filling and assembly, spread the ice cream into the prepared pie shell until it is almost full. Drizzle the Kahlúa over the top. Spread the prepared sauce over the ice cream layer. Sprinkle with the almonds. Freeze until firm. To serve, cut into slices and top with whipped topping.

Yield: 8 servings

BUTTER PECAN TARTS

Sweet enough for an elegant ending to a dinner party, but light enough for a morning coffee. These may be prepared early in the day for a party, and then stored at room temperature.

3 ounces cream cheese, softened
7 tablespoons butter or margarine, softened
1 cup flour
3/4 cup packed brown sugar
1 teaspoon vanilla extract

1 egg
1 tablespoon butter or margarine, softened
Pinch of salt
2/3 cup chopped pecans

Beat the cream cheese and 7 tablespoons butter at high speed in a mixing bowl until creamy. Reduce the speed to low and add the flour; beat until well blended. The dough should be very soft.

Divide the dough into 24 pieces. Press the dough pieces into the bottom and up the side of 24 miniature muffin cups. Make sure your fingertips are well floured.

Mix the brown sugar, vanilla, egg, 1 tablespoon butter and salt in a bowl with a fork or whisk. Place 1/2 the pecans in the bottom of the pastry-lined muffin cups. Spoon the filling by heaping teaspoons into each pastry cup. Sprinkle the remaining pecans over the tops.

Bake at 350 degrees for 30 minutes or until the filling is set and the edges of the crusts are golden brown. Loosen the tarts from the muffin cups and remove to a wire rack to cool. Store in an airtight container for up to 1 week.

Yield: 2 dozen

BUTTERSCOTCH SUNDAE MARTINI

Combine 1 ounce Godiva white chocolate liqueur, 1 ounce

butterscotch schnapps, 1 ounce Frangelico, 1 ounce amaretto

and 2 ounces premium vodka in a cocktail shaker.

Add crushed ice, cover and shake vigorously. Strain into

chilled martini glasses. Yield: 2 servings.

SWEET ALMOND SQUARES

Our tasters raved about these! They can be served in small pieces for a pick-up dessert or as a larger serving on an individual plate garnished with fruit for a shower or luncheon.

PASTRY

1/2 cup (1 stick) cold butter	1 tablespoon water
1 cup flour	

FILLING

1 cup water	3 eggs
1/2 cup (1 stick) butter	1 teaspoon almond extract
1 cup flour	

FROSTING

2 cups sifted confectioners' sugar	1 egg
1/4 cup (1/2 stick) butter, softened	1/2 teaspoon almond extract
	Sliced almonds

For the pastry, cut the butter into the flour in a bowl with a pastry blender or 2 knives until crumbly. Add the water and mix with your fingers until a dough forms. Divide the dough into 2 balls. Pat out each ball onto a baking sheet to make 2 long strips; set aside.

For the filling, heat the water and butter to boiling in a large saucepan. Remove from the heat and immediately beat in the flour until smooth. Add the eggs 1 at a time, beating to a smooth paste-like consistency. Stir in the almond extract. Spread the filling over the 2 pastry strips. Bake at 375 degrees for 40 minutes; let cool.

For the frosting, beat the confectioners' sugar, butter, egg and almond extract in a mixing bowl until smooth and of spreadable consistency.

To assemble, frost the tops of the baked strips when cool. Sprinkle the tops with the sliced almonds. Cut into strips to serve.

Note: To avoid raw eggs that may carry salmonella, we suggest using an equivalent amount of pasteurized egg substitute.

Yield: 12 servings

DOUBLE-CHOCOLATE SHORTBREAD

We don't believe there is such a thing as too much chocolate, which is why we included these delectable cookies. As part of a dessert tray or with a cappuccino, they are a rich treat. They make a festive presentation when cut into the shape of hearts.

1^1/2 cups flour	1 cup (2 sticks) unsalted butter,
^{1}/4 cup cornstarch	softened
^{1}/4 cup baking cocoa	^{1}/2 teaspoon almond extract
^{1}/4 teaspoon salt	^{3}/4 cup mini chocolate chips
1 cup confectioners' sugar	

Combine the flour, cornstarch, baking cocoa and salt in a bowl. Beat the sugar and butter in a mixing bowl until light and fluffy. Mix in the almond extract. Add the flour mixture and beat until well blended. Fold in the chocolate chips. Shape the dough into a disk. Wrap in plastic wrap and chill until firm. Roll out ^{1}/4 inch thick on a lightly floured surface. Cut into rounds using a 2-inch round cookie cutter. Place about 1 inch apart on a parchment-lined cookie sheet. Bake at 325 degrees for 8 to 10 minutes or until set and firm to the touch. Cool on wire racks.

Yield: 2 dozen

BRANDY ICE

Combine 2 quarts softened vanilla ice cream, 2 cups milk, ^{1}/3 cup brandy and 2 tablespoons crème de cacao in a blender. Process until very smooth. Pour into glasses and sprinkle with nutmeg to serve.

Yield: 6 to 8 servings

THE BEST BROWNIES

We had big expectations for these brownies and they certainly lived up to their name. Our submitter worked for years to perfect this recipe. The fruits of her labor give you a brownie for any occasion.

BASIC BROWNIE BATTER

3^{1}/$_{2}$ ounces unsweetened chocolate

^{3}/$_{4}$ cup (1^{1}/$_{2}$ sticks) unsalted butter, softened

1^{1}/$_{2}$ cups sugar

^{3}/$_{4}$ teaspoon vanilla extract

3 eggs

^{3}/$_{4}$ cup plus 2 tablespoons flour

^{1}/$_{4}$ teaspoon salt

^{1}/$_{2}$ cup plus 2 tablespoons chopped pecans, toasted (optional)

CARAMEL PECAN BROWNIES

7 ounces (^{1}/$_{2}$ bag) caramel candies, unwrapped

2 tablespoons heavy cream

1 cup (6 ounces) chocolate chips

1 cup chopped pecans

ESPRESSO CHOCOLATE CHUNK BROWNIES

1^{1}/$_{2}$ tablespoons espresso granules

1 cup chocolate chunks

For basic brownie batter, melt the chocolate and butter in a double boiler; cool. Add the sugar and vanilla and beat with an electric mixer until well blended. Add the eggs 1 at a time, beating well after each addition. Add the flour and salt and beat on low until well blended. Stir in ^{1}/$_{2}$ cup pecans. Spread the batter into a greased 8×8-inch baking pan. Sprinkle the remaining 2 tablespoons pecans over the top. Bake at 350 degrees for 30 minutes or until a wooden pick inserted in the center comes out with moist crumbs. Cool for 1 hour before cutting. For the best flavor, serve the next day.

For Caramel Pecan Brownies, prepare the Basic Brownie Batter as directed above, omitting the pecans. Heat the caramels and cream in a heavy saucepan over low heat until melted, stirring constantly until smooth. Pour ^{1}/$_{2}$ of the prepared brownie batter into the pan. Bake at 350 degrees for 10 to 12 minutes. Pour the hot caramel mixture over the brownie layer. Sprinkle with the chocolate chips and pecans. Pour the remaining ^{1}/$_{2}$ of the brownie batter over the top, spreading to cover evenly. Bake at 350 degrees for 15 minutes. Cool completely before cutting.

For Espresso Chocolate Chunk Brownies, prepare the Basic Brownie Batter as directed above, omitting the pecans. Mix in the espresso granules and chocolate chunks. Bake as directed for basic brownies.

Yield: 2 to 3 dozen small brownies

FROSTED PEANUT BUTTER BROWNIES

These brownies have the perfect sweet and salty balance. Kids, husbands, and neighbors raved about these when they were tested. Great to serve at your next barbeque, picnic, or just because you need them!

1 cup (2 sticks) butter
1/3 cup baking cocoa
2 cups sugar
1 1/2 cups flour
1/2 teaspoon salt
4 eggs
1 teaspoon vanilla extract
1 (18-ounce) jar crunchy peanut butter
1/2 cup (1 stick) butter
1/3 cup milk
10 large marshmallows
1/4 cup baking cocoa
1 (1-pound) package confectioners' sugar

Heat 1 cup butter and 1/3 cup baking cocoa in a saucepan over low heat until the butter melts, stirring constantly. Remove from the heat and cool. Mix the sugar, flour and salt in a large mixing bowl. Add the chocolate mixture and beat at medium speed until well blended. Add the eggs 1 at a time, beating well after each addition. Mix in the vanilla. Spread the batter into a 10×15-inch jelly roll pan. Bake at 350 degrees for 20 minutes or until a wooden pick inserted in the center comes out clean.

Remove the lid from the peanut butter jar. Microwave on Medium for 2 minutes, stirring after 1 minute. Spread over the warm brownies. Chill for 30 minutes.

Heat 1/2 cup butter, milk and marshmallows in a saucepan over medium heat until the marshmallows melt, stirring occasionally. Remove from the heat and whisk in 1/4 cup baking cocoa. Stir in the confectioners' sugar gradually, until the frosting is smooth and of spreadable consistency. Spread over the peanut butter layer. Chill for 20 minutes. Cut into squares to serve.

Yield: 2 to 3 dozen

PINEAPPLE DELIGHTS

Something different and fruity for a dessert tray or brunch dessert.

1 (2-layer) package yellow cake mix
1/2 cup (1 stick) butter or margarine, chilled
1 egg, beaten
1 (20-ounce) can crushed pineapple
3 tablespoons cornstarch
12 ounces cream cheese, softened
2 eggs
1 (1-pound) package confectioners' sugar

Process the cake mix and butter in a food processor until crumbly or combine in a bowl using 2 knives or fingers. Mix in the egg and press into the bottom of a greased 9×13-inch baking pan. Bake at 350 degrees for 10 minutes or until golden brown. Combine the undrained pineapple and cornstarch in a saucepan over low heat. Cook until thickened. Pour over the cake mix layer. Beat the cream cheese, 2 eggs and confectioners' sugar in a mixing bowl until smooth. Pour over the pineapple layer. Bake at 350 degrees for 35 to 45 minutes or until the center is set; cool. Chill until firm. Cut into squares to serve.

Yield: 24 bars

AMARETTO FREEZE

Combine 2 scoops vanilla ice cream, 1 1/2 ounces amaretto,

1/4 ounce Frangelica, 1/2 ounce half-and-half and 1/2 scoop crushed

ice in a blender. Process until smooth. Pour into glasses

and sprinkle with nutmeg to serve. Yield: 4 servings.

GUAVA CHEESE SQUARES

Guava is a popular fruit and flavoring in Cuban food. If you grew up on these, we hope this leads you down a sweet memory lane. You will find the cheese for this recipe in tubs in the dairy case of your grocery.

1/4 pound Merkt's Cheddar
cheese spread
1 1/2 cups flour
1 1/2 tablespoons brown sugar

1/2 cup (1 stick) butter, softened
Dash of salt
1 cup guava jelly

Combine the Cheddar cheese spread, flour, brown sugar, butter and salt in a food processor. Process until crumbly. You may also mix with a pastry blender in a bowl. Press 2/3 of the mixture into a greased 8×8-inch baking pan. Spread the guava jelly evenly over the top. Sprinkle the remaining mixture over the jelly, pressing into the jelly gently. Bake at 325 degrees for 30 minutes. Cool and cut into squares.

Yield: 12 servings

LIME MACADAMIA BARS

This is a variation on one of our favorite treats, the lemon bar. See if you agree that these are a tasty twist with lime and nuts.

2 cups flour
1/2 cup packed brown sugar
1 cup macadamia nuts, chopped
6 tablespoons (3/4 stick) butter
1/2 teaspoon salt

4 eggs
1 1/2 cups sugar
1/4 cup flour
1/2 cup plus 2 tablespoons fresh
lime juice

Combine 2 cups flour, the brown sugar, macadamia nuts, butter and salt in a food processor. Process until crumbly. Press into the bottom of a lightly greased 9×13-inch baking pan. Bake at 350 degrees for 15 to 20 minutes or until light brown.

Beat the eggs, sugar, 1/4 cup flour and lime juice in a mixing bowl. Pour over the warm crust. Bake at 350 degrees for 20 to 25 minutes or until the center is set. Cool and dust with confectioners' sugar. Cut into bars to serve.

Yield: 2 dozen bars

TROPICAL LAYER BARS

Imagine a seven-layer bar with tropical nuts and creamy caramel nougat throughout. Beware—these are very rich. We recommend cutting into very small squares for a dessert tray or serving with coffee or espresso after Bunco or book club.

1 box graham crackers, finely crushed
3/4 cup (1 1/2 sticks) butter, melted
1/2 cup sugar
3 cups (18 ounces) chocolate chips
2 cups flaked coconut
2 cups (4 sticks) butter
1 cup light corn syrup or honey
3 cups packed brown sugar
1/4 cup heavy cream
1 teaspoon vanilla extract
5 cups chopped macadamia nuts

Combine the crushed graham crackers, 3/4 cup melted butter and sugar in a bowl and mix well. Press into the bottom of an 11x17-inch baking pan. Sprinkle evenly with the chocolate chips and coconut.

Combine 2 cups butter, corn syrup and brown sugar in a heavy saucepan. Cook over low heat until the butter is melted, stirring with a wooden spoon. Increase the heat and bring to a boil for 3 minutes. Remove from the heat and stir in the cream, vanilla and macadamia nuts. Pour over the chocolate chip and coconut layer.

Bake at 350 degrees for 25 minutes or until the center is set. Cool completely. Chill until firm. Cut into small bars to serve.

Yield: 7 dozen small squares

SPECIAL THANKS

A cookbook is a collaboration of many people. To all those listed here, we thank you sincerely for your part in this endeavor. We have made every effort to express our gratitude to everyone who has touched this project. If we have inadvertently left your name out, please accept our sincere apologies.

To the families who so graciously gave us access to their beautiful homes for the photos in this cookbook:

Gael and John Carter
Mary Lee Nunnally Farrior
The Ferman Family
Gail and Arnold Levine
Molly and Jim Resch

To the businesses that allowed us access to props and settings for photographs in the cookbook:

Neiman Marcus, International Plaza—
china, crystal, serving pieces, accessories
HSN
Red Country Cottage nonstick cast-iron cookware (Bunco photo),
kitchen studio space (www.hsn.com)
Rent All of Tampa—
tables, table coverings, chairs, plates
Rosemary Cottage Tea Room—
baby quilts, Moses basket, baby washcloths, bunny (Baby Shower photo)
Villa Rosa Distinctive Linens & Bath Shop—
baby shower packages

RECIPE CONTRIBUTORS

A special thank you to our many recipe contributors, who submitted their treasured recipes and favorite foods. Although we could not use them all, each was unique and wonderful . . .

Brooke Alexander
Laura Allegri
Lisa Andrews
Stephanie Andrews
JoEllen Archerd
Anne Arthur
Julie Atkinson
Tammy Augen
April Ayers
Tracy Bales
Jean Barrett
Cheryl Benitez
Lindsey Bettendorf
Nancy Blake
Lisa Blowers
Alexis Borucke
Patricia Bowker
Katherine Boyet
Tiffany Brandt
Anne Harper Brewer
Laura Brooks
Chris Holt Brown
Helen T. Brown
Michelle Capitano
Ashley Carl
Virginia Charest
Tracy Clouser
Kathy Conner
Ann Cox
Laurie Doerr Daigle
Joy Culverhouse
   Daugherty
Mary Deemer
Connie Detrick
Penny Dewell
Israel Diaz
Mary Beth Dickinson

Patricia Dignam
   Donaldson
Laura Farrior
Cheryl Fraser
Joanne Frazier
Lisa Gabler
Rebecca Jo Garbrick
Beth Garcia
Wendy Garraty
Ashley Germain
Karla Gibson
Laura Lee Glass
Clara Gough
Betsy Graham
Sarah Green
Sue Greene
Jan Gruetzmacher
Lynn Guilford
Donna Hall
Kathy Hansen
Kim Harcrow
Elizabeth Harris
Caroline Hatton
Vicki Hayes
Catherine Healy
Cyrilla Helm
Chandra Henthorne
Megan Hernandez
Michelle Hogan
Mary Hulse
Joelle Hunter
Sue Isbell
Nina Jennings
Kristen Karig-Day
Lynn P. Reynolds Keel
Patricia King
Carol LoCicero Kline

Susan Knight
Lynn Koeniger
Jessie Krusen
Elizabeth Krystyn
Brenda Kusak
Deanna Laird
Tiffany Larson
Dara Leslie
Susan Lienhart
Jennifer Lima-Smith
Ann Lindell
Valerie Litschgi
Heather Logue
Mary Alice Lopez
Lorena Hart Ludovici
Judy Marks
Maryanne McDonough
Jennifer McQueen
Lisa McRae
Phyllis Mitchell
Cameron Bryant
   Monroe
Melissa Morrow
Mindy Murphy
Nancy Mynard
Patricia L. Nobel
Mary Ellen Norton
Mimi Obeck
Jennifer Olinley
Jennifer Ownby
Martha Park
Mary Persky
Christine Phillips
Natasha Phillips
Shannon Piefer
Vanessa Fava Pivec
Julie Pizzo

Sharon Smith Pizzo
Kathleen Purdy
Audrie Ranon
Allison Reddick
Christie Romer
Dianne Rossi
Pam Rush
Brittany Rustman
Carla Saavedra
Kristie Salzer
Michelle Schofner
Lisa Elkim Schwartz
Mary Jo Shenk
Despina Sibley
Linda Smith
Angie Sparks
Jennifer M. Stauffer
Susan Steele
Janice Straske
Amy Tamargo
Victoria Thaxton
Lynda Triplett
Leanne Voiland
Christina Volini
Mignyon Warren
Teresa Weachter
Missy Weiner
Danielle Welsh
Elizabeth Whiteley
Andrea Wilkinson
Carol Wilkinson
Stacy Williams
Lori Wilson
Mary S. Wolfe
Barbara Woods
Laura York

RECIPE TESTERS

With appreciation to our faithful testers who opened their kitchens and gave us invaluable feedback . . .

Brooke Alexander
Jan Anderson
Lisa Andrews
Tami Augen
Anne Bartlett
Cheryl Benitez
Elizabeth Bettendorf
Hedy Bever
Laura W. Billings
Nancy Blake
Lisa Blowers
Alexis Borucke
Katherine Boyet
Heather Brock
Laura Brooks
Helen T. Brown
Pam Calary
Theresa Cannella
Melinda Cashin
Ginny Charest
Lisa Clark
Laurie Doerr Daigle
Kristen Day
Robin DeLaVergne
Terrie Dodson
Laura Farrior
Meg Fernandez
Cheryl Fraser
Joanne Frazier
Katherine Frazier
Laura Darrow Frost
Lisa Gabler
Beth Garcia
Laura Gauthier
Clara Gough

Betsy Graham
Sue Greene
Cindy Hadlow
Cynthia Hahmann
Donna Hall
Elizabeth Harris
Cyrilla Helm
Michelle Hogan
Nina Jennings
Kim Keiper
Carole King
Shannon King
Lynne Koeniger
Deanna Laird
Pam LaPan
Dara Leslie
Irene Martinez
Tracy McBride
Maryanne McDonough
Joan McKay
Julianne McKeel
Laurie McLamore
Jennifer McQueen
Lisa McRae
Brooke Melendi
Cammie Monroe
Melissa Morrow
Kim Murphy
Mindy Murphy
Nancy H. Mynard
Mimi Obeck
Lori Pucci-Rey
Kathleen Purdy
Audrie Ranon
Carla Saavedra

Kristie Salzer
Mary Jo Shenk
Angie Sparks
Anita Spofford
Lynn Stanford
Susan Steele
Lisa Strader
Sue Strand
Janice Straske
Becky Suberly
Amy Tamargo
Ann VonThron
Laine Walker
Laura Walsh
Teresa Weachter
Missy Weiner
Danielle Welsh
Virginia Wilson
Jenny Wilwant
Pat Wood
Lou Yates

INDEX

THE LIFE *of the* PARTY

The Junior League of Tampa, Inc.
87 Columbia Drive
Tampa, Florida 33606
813-254-1734 extension 502
www.jltampa.org

YOUR ORDER	QUANTITY	TOTAL
The Life of the Party at $17.95 per book		$
JLT Cookbook Collection at $44.95 (includes *The Life of the Party*, *Tampa Treasures*, and *Gasparilla* cookbooks)		$
Florida residents add 7% sales tax per book		$
Shipping and handling at $4.95 for one book; $2.00 for each additional book		$
UPS next day delivery available upon request	TOTAL	$

Name _____

Address _____

City _____ State _____ Zip _____

Telephone _____

Method of Payment: [ ] VISA   [ ] MasterCard
                    [ ] Check payable to Junior League of Tampa

Account Number _____ Expiration Date _____

Signature _____

Photocopies will be accepted.